"[Lee Camp is] developing a reputation for fearless political comedy, with some calling him an heir to the crown of the late, great George Carlin. He gets our seal of approval."
—*Time Out Sydney*

"Gets the crowd roaring!"
—*Rolling Stone*

"A Time-Bomb of Reason ready to destroy anything that seeks to pollute our culture and restrict our possibility as a species."
—Peter Joseph (creator of *The Zeitgeist Movement*)

"Lee Camp can be devastating."
—NPR's *Weekend Edition*

"Some of the best satire I've seen."
—Scott Dikkers, cofounder and former editor of the *Onion*

"Lee has one of the funniest shows on television. I watch it every week."
—Jesse Ventura, former governor of Minnesota

"One of a handful of comedians keeping my father's torch lit."
—Kelly Carlin, daughter of George Carlin

"Lee Camp is not just a comedian. He challenges the corporate war narratives and calls out the American empire's bullshit better than anyone. His passion and anger are infectious and far too rare."
—Abby Martin, journalist, host of *The Empire Files*, former host of *Breaking the Set*

"Lee Camp is a rare prophetic voice in a field of formulaic blowhards and political opportunists. He has the unique ability to tear our political establishment to shreds, and to then smash those shreds with a righteous hammer until we see the elite forces that rule our lives in their truest form—as an utterly hilarious farce of bipartisan idiocy."
—Max Blumenthal, journalist, author of *Goliath*

"There is no better voice to analyze the bizarre combination of absurdity and catastrophe facing us today than that of Lee Camp. Drawing on his experience in both satire and politics, Camp uses his critical insight and sharp sense of irony to offer readers compelling political commentary that is as powerful as it is witty."
—Sophia McClennan, author of *Is Satire Saving Our Nation? Mockery and American Politics*, professor of International Affairs and Comparative Literature at Penn State University, and founding director of the Center for Global Studies

"Lee Camp has found the hole in America's brain where reason has been replaced by Walmart. Lee's rants channel the gunk oozing out. You have to admit, that's why he's so fucking funny."
—Greg Palast, journalist, author of *The Best Democracy Money Can Buy*

"Camp's show is a master class in politically driven comedy. Razor-sharp, witty, acerbic, and somewhat off-the-wall at times, he delivers his on-point political and social messages with the biggest dollop of humor going."
—Steven Topple, *The Canary*

"Incisive humor that inspires both bouts of uncontrollable laughter and moments of reflection about the country's troubling political realities."
—Whitney Webb, *Mint Press News*

"For those comedy fans still in mourning for Bill Hicks, you'll find plenty to enjoy in the work of DC-born stand-up Lee Camp."
—*The Guardian*

"Like Jon Stewart from the *Daily Show* but with sharper teeth."
—*The Herald*

"Lee Camp is an integral part of a long-standing satirical tradition. He has the rare ability to make you laugh and think simultaneously."
—Paul Krassner, satirist

"Lee is the Che Guevara of comedy. Congrats to him on his balls and integrity. Everything he does is *so* good. We need more comedians with his kind of fearlessness. It's so rare to find such artful, thoughtful passion in comedy these days . . . or in life. He's waiting for a generation to catch up with him."
—Paul Provenza, comedian, filmmaker, *The Aristocrats*

"Lee is totally inspiring. I kinda wanna be like him when I grow up."
—Rain Pryor, actor, comedian, daughter of Richard Pryor

BULLET POINTS AND PUNCH LINES

Lee Camp

Bullet Points and Punch Lines
by Lee Camp
©Lee Camp
This edition © 2020 PM Press

ISBN: 978–1–62963–785–3 (paperback)
ISBN: 978–1–62963–821–8 (hardcover)
ISBN: 978–1–62963–802–7 (ebook)

Library of Congress Control Number: 2019945900

Cover by John Yates / www.stealworks.com
Photo by Deneka Peniston
Interior design by briandesign

10 9 8 7 6 5 4 3 2 1

PM Press
PO Box 29312
Oakland, CA 94623
www.pmpress.org

Printed in the USA

CONTENTS

Many of the following columns first appeared on Truthdig or as monologues on my show *Redacted Tonight with Lee Camp* on RT America. While several wonderful editors have made small changes, I wrote every piece myself. So if you love the book, please give me all the credit. If you hate it, blame the editors.

This book wouldn't have been possible without the help and support of many people at RT America and Truthdig, Eleanor Goldfield, John F. O'Donnell, Naomi Karavani, Natalie McGill, Yoki Danoff, Rhys Baker, Michele Greenstein, Abby Martin, and the millions of people fighting for peace, sustainability, and equality around the world.

Things always seem most desperate and hopeless just before large-scale change. . . . Keep fighting.

—Lee Camp

FOREWORD

by Chris Hedges

In his essay "Shooting an Elephant," George Orwell wrote that power for the ruling elites entails "one long struggle not to be laughed at." Withering criticism and cogent analysis of their crimes and peculiarities they can stomach. But when the entire ruling class is reduced to ridicule, when the very presence of the elites evokes derisive laughter, the powerful shrink in size before our eyes. Stripped of pomp and power, they become clowns. And once they are transformed into clowns, they become ruthless.

There are two types of comics. There are those who focus on the foibles and excesses of the powerful, and there are those, such as Lee Camp and Jimmy Dore, as well as the late George Carlin, who focus on how the powerful are the public face of oppression and exploitation.

Comics who take aim at buffoonish figures like Donald Trump have little to fear. Trump or Jeff Sessions or any of the other half-wits in the White House are an embarrassment to the ruling elites. Trump and his coterie of imbecilic enablers provide daily fodder for mainstream comics, who night after night hold up their absurdities and gaffes and studiously ignore the crimes of the corporate systems that makes them rich.

Those comics who take aim at the entire ruling establishment, who are as withering about Barack Obama and Hillary Clinton as about Trump, who expose them all as hypocrites and puppets of global capitalism and imperialism, are swiftly marginalized, demonized, and censored. The followers of these types of comics are blocked on Facebook and YouTube, something Camp and Dore have experienced. These comics, the ruling elite understands, are dangerous. They expose the nature of power itself. They damn and ridicule all who serve the system. And totalitarian regimes, including our system of corporate totalitarianism, are often more frightened of these artists, who have a mass appeal, than writers like me whose analysis of the system is not much different from radical comics but who do not turn this analysis into biting satire and humor.

The language of satire, which Camp uses effectively in his shows and his writing, is often more successful in exposing reality.

Here is Camp, for example, on how the Pentagon cannot account for how it spent 21 trillion dollars:

> There are certain things the human mind is not meant to do. Our complex brains cannot view the world in infrared, cannot spell words backwards during orgasm, and cannot *really* grasp numbers over a few thousand. A few thousand we can feel and conceptualize. We've all been in stadiums with several thousand people. We have an idea of what that looks like (and how sticky the floor gets).
>
> But when we get into the millions, we lose it. It becomes a fog of nonsense. Visualizing it feels like trying to hug a memory. We may know what one million dollars can buy (and we may want that thing), but you probably don't know how tall a stack of a million one-dollar bills is. You probably don't know how long it takes a minimum-wage employee to make one million dollars.
>
> That's why trying to understand—truly understand—that the Pentagon spent 21 trillion unaccounted

for dollars between 1998 and 2015 washes over you like
your mother telling you that your third cousin you met
twice is getting divorced. It seems vaguely upsetting,
but you forget about it 15 seconds later because . . .
what else is there to do?

Twenty-one trillion.

This kind of comic writing captures the outrage we
should all feel about 21 trillion dollars in waste and fraud by
the Pentagon. It repeatedly hammers home outrage through
humor. Its clever verbal repetition does not allow us to glide
over the number. We are forced to grasp its enormity. And,
as Camp points out, the Democratic Party is as complicit in
this debacle as the Republican Party. There is no way at this
level to separate Trump from Obama. One may be vulgar
and brash, but the other uses urbane polish to accomplish
the same ends.

It is vital that corporate power maintains the fiction of
a difference. It does this by reducing politics to political per-
sonalities. When writers or comics expose the true nature of
the beast itself, then the ruling elites use everything at their
disposal to discredit them. This is why the *New York Times* and
NPR have devoted inordinate time and space to attacking
Camp, a comic whom I expect many readers of the *New York
Times* and listeners to NPR do not know. The elites, who keep
Camp on the margins of the media landscape, however, want
to be the first to define and defame him, just in case. They
want to make sure he remains a pariah.

Camp and other radical comics are often able to reach
people that writers such as myself will never reach. They are
an important gateway into our reality, using humor and satire
like a weapon to rip back the veil on the dirty machinations of
power. We cannot underestimate their cultural importance,
their power, or how much the elites are determined to silence
them because they are comics. And that is why Camp is a
cultural treasure.

INTRODUCTION

by Jimmy Dore

People need truth.

They need it like oxygen.

The American people have been suffocating on lies.

Lee Camp is providing a much needed Heimlich maneuver.

Lee targets the putrid pundits, capitalist scum, fascist freaks, socially acceptable war criminals, double-talking liberal elites, and the useless corporate media that enables them.

The first time I saw Lee Camp was on Fox News. It was during that era of Fox News hosts writing books with titles like *Shut Up and Sing* (which I didn't know was technically possible).[1] Lee was in the studio among the pointless pundits and brain-dead teleprompter readers. I was immediately envious of his opulent Jesus-like hair. Lee punctured the empty noise with the observation that Fox News was "a parade of propaganda, a festival of ignorance." This put the network into a frantic hysteria as they cut to their next segment, detailing how Captain Kirk seduced hot alien chicks. (I'm not kidding.)

Lee was doing what he does best—speaking truth to power. This is the highest calling of the comedian.

I've been a fan ever since . . . and I'm still envious of his hair.

Rulers were made to be broken. Lee does not take part in the theater of political parties jostling for power. He understands that the struggle is not left vs. right. The struggle is top vs. bottom.

When I say we need to cut off the top, it isn't another reference to hair.

Because Lee is not partisan, he is even more dangerous to establishment power, but that also leaves him vulnerable. When power is attacked with the truth, the only retaliation option left to them is slander.

Case in point: the New York Times did a smear piece about Lee, linking him to conspiracy theorists with baseless intimations. I feel an immediate affinity to anyone smeared by the New York Times, because if I were praised by the organization that fired Pulitzer Prize–winning reporter Chris Hedges for telling the truth about the Iraq War, I would know I was doing something wrong with my work.

The New York Times article was an absurd attempt to discredit Lee's scorching critiques of corporate power with the familiar jealousy over Lee's hair (though this fails to explain what happened to Chris Hedges). That article's claims eventually had to be retracted.

We are living in crisis—a crisis of inequality, a crisis of climate disaster, a crisis of democracy. The stenographers to power won't acknowledge it, as they cash their checks and lick boots. I get annoyed at TV news programs interrupting the commercials. The acting is usually better on the commercials, though the old actor pretending to love his catheter was almost as believable as Brian Williams pretending to be a reporter.

As the oligarchs try to squeeze out the remaining blood money from the last gasps of empire, the voices of dissidents like Lee Camp are more important than ever. Using his scathing wit and unflinching eye for bullshit, he shames all conformists and sycophants.

Sometimes when I'm waiting in line to purchase a chemical-laced genetically modified turnip from a cashier who is a single mom working three jobs to buy her blood pressure medication and pay off her student debt, while her child is overseas serving in the military to steal the natural resources of a foreign nation, I find myself asking, "Why don't more people know Lee Camp's work?"

Slowly I realize the answer: if more people knew Lee Camp's work, he would have to be "Assange-ed." If that day comes, we'll just need to read the following pages to find out who did it.

NOTES

1   Laura Ingraham, *Shut Up and Sing: How Elites from Hollywood, Politics, and the Media Are Subverting America* (Washington, DC: Regnery Publishing, 2006).

THE PENTAGON CAN'T ACCOUNT FOR 21 TRILLION DOLLARS (THAT'S NOT A TYPO)

Twenty-one trillion dollars.

The Pentagon's own numbers show that it can't account for 21 trillion dollars. Yes, I mean trillion with a "T." And this could change everything.

But I'll get back to that in a moment.

There are certain things the human mind is not meant to do. Our complex brains cannot view the world in infrared, cannot spell words backwards during orgasm, and cannot *really* grasp numbers over a few thousand. A few thousand we can feel and conceptualize. We've all been in stadiums with several thousand people. We have an idea of what that looks like (and how sticky the floor gets).

But when we get into the millions, we lose it. It becomes a fog of nonsense. Visualizing it feels like trying to hug a memory. We may know what one million dollars can buy (and we may want that thing), but you probably don't know how tall a stack of a million one-dollar bills is. You probably don't know how long it takes a minimum-wage employee to make one million dollars.

That's why trying to understand—truly understand—that the Pentagon spent 21 trillion unaccounted for dollars between 1998 and 2015 washes over you like your mother telling you that your third cousin you met twice is getting divorced.[1] It seems vaguely upsetting, but you forget about it 15 seconds later because . . . what else is there to do?

Twenty-one trillion.

But let's get back to the beginning. A couple of years ago, Mark Skidmore, an economics professor, heard Catherine Austin Fitts, former assistant secretary in the Department of Housing and Urban Development, say that the Department of Defense Office of Inspector General had found 6.5 trillion dollars worth of unaccounted for spending in 2015.[2] Skidmore, being an economics professor, thought something like, "She means 6.5 billion dollars. Not trillion. Because trillion would mean the Pentagon couldn't account for more money than the gross domestic product of the whole United Kingdom. But still, 6.5 billion dollars of unaccounted for money is a crazy amount."

So he went and looked at the inspector general's report, and he found something interesting: it was *trillion!*[3] It was fucking 6.5 trillion dollars of unaccounted for spending in 2015! And I'm sorry for the cursing, but it's legally obligatory to preface the word "trillion" with "fucking." It is indeed way more than the UK's GDP.

Skidmore did a little more digging. As *Forbes* reported in December 2017, "[He] and Catherine Austin Fitts . . . conducted a search of government websites and found similar reports dating back to 1998. While the documents are incomplete, original government sources indicate $21 trillion in unsupported adjustments have been reported for the Department of Defense and the Department of Housing and Urban Development for the years 1998–2015."[4]

Let's stop and take a second to conceive how much 21 trillion dollars is (which we can't, because our brains short-circuit, but we'll try anyway).

- The amount of money supposedly in the stock market is 30 trillion dollars.[5]
- The GDP of the United States is 20.5 trillion dollars.[6]

- Picture a stack of money. Now imagine that that stack of dollars is all one-thousand-dollar bills. Each bill says "$1,000" on it. How high do you imagine that stack of bills would be if it were *one trillion dollars*. It would be 63 miles high.[7]
- Imagine you make 40 thousand dollars a year. How long would it take you to make one trillion dollars? Well, don't sign up for this task, because it would take you 25 million years (which sounds like a long time, but I hear that the last 10 million really fly by, because you already know your way around the office, where the coffee machine is, etc.).

The human brain is not meant to think about a trillion dollars.

And it's definitely not meant to think about the 21 trillion dollars our Department of Defense can't account for. These numbers sound bananas. They sound like something Alex Jones found tattooed on his backside by extraterrestrials.

But the 21 trillion number comes from the Department of Defense Office of Inspector General—the OIG. Although, as *Forbes* pointed out, "after Mark Skidmore began inquiring about OIG-reported unsubstantiated adjustments, the OIG's webpage, which documented, albeit in a highly incomplete manner, these unsupported 'accounting adjustments,' was mysteriously taken down."

Luckily, people had already grabbed copies of the report, which—for now—you can view here.[8]

Here's something else important from that *Forbes* article—which is one of the only mainstream media articles you can find on the largest theft in American history: "Given that the entire Army budget in fiscal year 2015 was $120 billion, unsupported adjustments were 54 times the level of spending authorized by Congress."

That's right. The expenses with *no explanation* were 54 times the actual budget allotted by Congress. Well, it's good to see Congress is doing 1/54th of its job of overseeing military spending. (That's actually more than I thought Congress was doing.) This would seem to mean that 98 percent of every dollar spent by the Army in 2015 was unconstitutional.

So, pray tell, what did the OIG say caused all this unaccounted for spending that makes Jeff Bezos's net worth look like that of a guy jingling a tin can on the street corner?

"[The July 2016 inspector general] report indicates that unsupported adjustments are the result of the Defense Department's 'failure to correct system deficiencies.'"

They blame *trillions of dollars* of mysterious spending on a "failure to correct system deficiencies"? That's like me saying I had sex with 100 thousand wild hairless aardvarks, because I wasn't looking where I was walking.

Twenty-one trillion.

Say it slowly to yourself.

At the end of the day, there are no justifiable explanations for this amount of unaccounted for, unconstitutional spending. Right now, the Pentagon is being audited for the first time ever,[9] and it's taking 2,400 auditors to do it. I'm not holding my breath that they'll actually be allowed to get to the bottom of this.

But if the American people truly understood this number, it would change both the country and the world. It means that the dollar is sprinting down a path toward worthlessness. If the Pentagon is hiding spending that dwarfs the amount of tax dollars coming in to the federal government, then it's clear the government is printing however much it wants and thinking there are no consequences. Once these trillions are considered, our fiat currency has even less meaning than it already did, and it's only a matter of time before inflation runs wild.

It also means that any time our government says it "doesn't have money" for a project, it's laughable. It can clearly "create" as much as it wants for bombing and death. This would explain how Donald Trump's military can drop well over 100 bombs a day that cost well north of one million dollars each.[10]

So why can't our government also "create" endless money for health care, education, the homeless, veterans' benefits, and the elderly, to make all parking free, and to pay the Rolling Stones to play stoop-front shows in my neighborhood? (I'm sure the Rolling Stones are expensive, but surely a trillion dollars could cover a couple of songs.)

Obviously, our government could do those things, but it chooses not to. Earlier this month, Louisiana sent eviction notices to 30 thousand elderly people on Medicaid, to kick them out of their nursing homes.[11] Yes, a country that can vomit trillions of dollars down a black hole marked "military" can't find the money to take care of our poor elderly. It's a repulsive joke.

Twenty-one trillion.

Former secretary of defense Robert Gates spoke about how no one knows where the money is flying in the Pentagon. In a barely reported speech in 2011, he said, "My staff and I learned that it was nearly impossible to get accurate information and answers to questions such as 'how much money did you spend' and 'how many people do you have?'"[12]

They can't even find out how many people work for a specific department?

Note for anyone looking for a job: just show up at the Pentagon and tell them you work there. It doesn't seem like they'd have much luck proving you don't.

For more on this story, check out David DeGraw's excellent reporting at ChangeMaker.media, because the mainstream corporate media are mouthpieces for the weapons industry. They are friends with benefits of the military-industrial complex. I have seen basically nothing from the mainstream corporate media concerning this mysterious 21 trillion dollars. I missed the time when CNN's Wolf Blitzer said that the money we dump into war and death—either the accounted for money or the secretive trillions—could end world hunger and poverty many times over.[13] There's no reason anybody needs to be starving or hungry or unsheltered on this planet, but our government seems hell-bent on proving that it stands for nothing but profiting off death and misery. And our media desperately want to show they stand for nothing but propping up our morally bankrupt empire.

When the media aren't actively promoting war, they're filling the airwaves with shit, so the entire country can't even hear itself think. Our whole mindscape is filled to the brim with nonsense and vacant celebrity idiocy. Then, while no one is looking, the largest theft humankind has ever seen is going on behind our backs—covered up under the guise of "national security."

Twenty-one trillion.

Don't forget.

NOTES

1   Laurence Kotlikoff, "Has Our Government Spent $21 Trillion of Our Money without Telling Us?" *Forbes*, December 8, 2017, accessed September 24, 2019, https://www.forbes.com/sites/kotlikoff/2017/12/08/has-our-government-spent-21-trillion-of-our-money-without-telling-us/#161e89207aef.

2   Ibid.

3   Inspector General, U.S. Department of Defense, *Army General Fund Adjustments Not Adequately Documented or Supported*, July 26, 2016, accessed September 24, 2019, https://media.defense.gov/2016/Jul/26/2001714261/-1/-1/1/DODIG-2016-113.pdf.

4   Kotlifoff, "Has Our Government Spent $21 Trillion of Our Money without Telling Us?"

5   Vito J. Racanelli, "The US Stock Market Is Now Worth $30 Trillion," *Barron's*, January 18, 2018, accessed September 24, 2019, https://www.barrons.com/articles/the-u-s-stock-market-is-now-worth-30-trillion-1516285704.

6   World Bank, "GDP (current $US)," accessed September 24, 2019, https://data.worldbank.org/indicator/NY.GDP.MKTP.CD.

7   "How Much Is a Trillion Dollars?" If I Had a Trillion Dollars Youth Film Festival, accessed September 24, 2019, https://ihtd.org/festivalguide/resources/how-much-is-a-trillion-dollars/.

8   Department of Defense Office of Inspector General, *Army General Fund Adjustments Not Adequately Documented or Supported*, July 26, 2016, accessed September 24, 2019, https://www.dodig.mil/reports.html/ Article/1119298/army-general-fund-adjustments-not-adequately-documented-or-supported/.

9   Bill Chappell, "Pentagon Announces First-Ever Audit of the Department of Defense," NPR, December 8, 2017, accessed September 24, 2019, https://www.npr.org/sections/thetwo-way/2017/12/08/569394885/ pentagon-announces-first-ever-audit-of-the-department-of-defense.

10 John Haltiwanger, "Trump Has Dropped Record Number of Bombs on Middle East," *Newsweek*, September 19, 2017, accessed September 24, 2019, http://www.newsweek.com/trump-era-record-number-bombs-dropped-middle-east-667505.

11 Greg Hilburn, "More than 30,000 Nursing Home Eviction Notices to Be Sent in Louisiana Thursday," *USA Today*, May 7, 2018, accessed September 24, 2019, https://www.usatoday.com/story/news/nation-now/2018/05/07/louisiana-nursing-home-eviction-notices-could-create-mass-chaos/588867002/.

12 Robert M. Gates, "Secretary of Defense Speech," U.S. Department of Defense, May 24, 2011, accessed September 24, 2019, https://archive. defense.gov/Speeches/Speech.aspx?SpeechID=1570.

13 Elisabeth Rosenthal and Andrew Martin, "UN Says Solving Food Crisis Could Cost $30 Billion," *New York Times*, June 4, 2008, accessed September 24, 2019, https://www.nytimes.com/2008/06/04/news/ 04iht-04food.13446176.html.

HOW TO CREATE A US-BACKED GOVERNMENT COUP FOR FUN AND PROFIT!

Nicaragua just defeated a US-backed violent coup attempt, and no one cares.

Well, let me revise that: very few care. English teachers may care, because they may find it fascinating that the phrase "violent coup" is one of the only English phrases often introduced with the prefix "US-backed."

But I can tell you for certain the mainstream media don't want you to care. They don't even want you to know it happened. And they certainly don't want you to know that it followed a simple formula for US-backed coups in leftist and anti-imperialist nations throughout Latin America, a formula our military intelligence apparatus has implemented in numerous countries tirelessly, like an overused football play.

On the corporate airwaves you won't hear about US-backed *anything*. If the US military backed up *a truck*, CNN wouldn't mention it, NPR would tell you the truck was dealing with an "organic internal protest movement," and Fox News would blame a black person.

For example, there's the US-backed genocide going on in Yemen right now.[1] As a recent Fairness and Accuracy in Reporting study made clear, over the 12 months prior to July 3, 2018, MSNBC aired a grand total of *zero* stories about Yemen,[2] while it spewed forth 455 stories about the porn star our president pooned (which is roughly 445 too many, even if you're *really* into presidential erotic fan fiction).

Back to Latin America. The US has long had a policy of undermining, infiltrating, and bringing down any Latin American government that doesn't line up with our unfettered capitalist neoliberal policies. If a leader says, "Hey, let's live a different way in which everyone is taken care of and we help out our brothers and sisters," then the US will make sure he or she ends up wearing cement shoes at the bottom of a lake somewhere. (And those cement shoes won't even be crafted by union cement workers, because all the unions have been destroyed. So you've got freelance underpaid children making the shoes—probably part of the "gig economy" with some sort of cement shoe app that tricks cement layers into working for pennies, because they don't understand the algorithm is screwing them *hard!*)

Anyway, Nicaragua is the latest US-backed attempted coup. So this seems like a good time to present: "How to Create a US-Backed Government Coup!"

You can play along at home—especially if your home is in Nicaragua or Venezuela.

Step One: Create a strong US-backed "fifth column."
Don't tell me you don't know what a "fifth column" is. How could you be so naive?! (This is the part where I mock you for lacking knowledge that I myself learned only last week.)

As smart person Peter Koenig explains, "A Fifth Column is a group of people who undermine the government of a country in support of the enemy. They can be both covert and open."[3]

There are various ways to create fifth columns. We here in the US like to create ours with a good, wholesome front: nonprofit organizations. Our two favorites are USAID and the National Endowment for Democracy (NED). What is the NED? Well, as editor of Consortium News Robert Parry put it, "In 1983, NED essentially took over the CIA's role of influencing electoral outcomes and destabilizing governments that got in the way of US interests, except that NED carried out those functions in a quasi-overt fashion while the CIA did them covertly. NED also serves as a sort of slush fund for neocons."[4]

(When I picture a neocon slush fund, I picture Dick Cheney, Mitch McConnell, and Bill Kristol naked in a small bathtub filled with the vomit of all their victims. Yes, it's gross. But it's less gross than what a neocon slush fund *really* is.)

So we use NED and USAID to destabilize countries. Keep in mind, though it may not sound like much, there are consequences to destabilizing countries. By doing so, we indirectly kill a lot of people, or at least ruin their lives, leaving them poor or destitute. But to create a successful coup, it's important you *don't care* about any of that stuff. Leave that for the nerds with their pencils and their statistics. If babies die because they can't get the medical treatment they need, not your problem. You've got other stuff to do—like wiping bird shit off your $1,200 loafers.

Step Two: Undermine the country's economy.
This can be done via sanctions, as we are currently doing in Venezuela and Iran.[5] Simultaneously, use the fifth column and the obedient American media hacks (CNN, Fox News, MSNBC) to convince the people of said country that their economic troubles are the fault of only their president. "It's the Venezuelan president's fault you don't have toilet paper! He's hoarding all the toilet paper. He's sitting up there on a throne made of Angel Soft triple-ply! His anus is singing 'Joy to the World' right now!"

But what our corporate media really don't want you to know is the truth. Peter Koenig, who was also an international observer for the Presidential Economic Advisory Commission (showoff), stated, "It is absolutely clear who is behind the food and medicine boycotts (empty supermarket shelves), and the induced internal violence [in Venezuela]. It is a carbon copy of what the CIA under Kissinger's command did in Chile in 1973, which led to the murder of the legitimate and democratically elected President Allende and to the Pinochet military coup."[6]

So you create economic troubles, which make people hungry and angry, and that leads to. . .

Step Three: Wait for internal protests and/or create them.

Basically, there were legitimate protests in Nicaragua, because what country *doesn't* have protests now and again? But then the US and our front groups threw kerosene on that fire. The NED-funded publication Global Americans actually bragged about the kerosene it threw. In an article titled "Laying the groundwork for insurrection: A closer look at the US role in Nicaragua's social unrest," it said, "the NED has funded 54 projects in Nicaragua between 2014 and 2017."[7]

Various US-backed groups redirected the protests against the Daniel Ortega government. Some protesting students were even flown to the United States for further instruction from Freedom House, which has deep ties to the CIA. Once here, the students posed for photos with none other than US Sen. Marco Rubio, R-Fla.[8]

If there's anyone I trust, it's people who are *proud* to meet Marco Rubio. I mean, even Marco Rubio's *kids* tell people that Joe Biden is their father.

So, as with Syria, after genuine protests began in Nicaragua, the US used the fifth column to exacerbate the tension and channel the protests toward a violent showdown.

Step Four: Get violent while accusing the government of getting violent.

We've seen this tactic in Nicaragua and Venezuela. There was violence on both sides of the protests but far more on the US-backed sides, sometimes with help from the CIA or alumni from our military training facilities like the School of the Americas.[9] But because of media propaganda, many believe there is primarily violence on the government side, when in fact it's the opposite.

Step Five: If steps one through four don't work, kidnap or assassinate.
The time may come when you've exhausted other options and simply must whack a dude. Don't feel bad. It happens to the best of us.

Or, if you're feeling generous, you can put said target on a US military plane and fly him to Africa against his will—as happened in 2004 to the president of Haiti, Jean-Bertrand Aristide. He was kidnapped by our military and taken on one of the most awkward 14-hour flights one can imagine.[10]

There are endless examples. Want some more? How about the 1973 CIA-backed overthrow and killing of socialist president Salvador Allende in Chile? But have no fear, he was replaced by murderous dictator Augusto Pinochet, whom the US liked *a lot* better. (We shared the same taste in death squads.)

Ecuadorean president Jaime Roldós Aguilera died in an airplane "accident" in 1981, after going forward with a plan to reorganize Ecuador's fossil fuel industry that US interests were very much against.[11] His airplane fell out of the sky after coming down with a bad case of the CIA.

Even NBC has recounted the bizarre CIA plots to assassinate Fidel Castro in Cuba, some of them involving exploding cigars.[12] To be honest, I can't look down on that, because it is the funniest way to kill someone. So as long as it gets a laugh, I approve.

And a few weeks ago, we saw an attempt to kill President Nicolás Maduro in Venezuela with a small explosive drone. While there's no indication the US military was directly involved, that's not really how it rolls. The military prefers to fund front groups so it looks like the US had nothing to do with it. And keep in mind there *was* a US-backed coup against Hugo Chávez, Maduro's predecessor, in 2002.[13] So taking out the Chávez-Maduro government has been a long-term goal of the US deep state.

There you have it—thanks for playing "How to Create a US-Backed Government Coup!"

Join us next week for "How to Create a US-Backed Cholera Outbreak! . . . starring Saudi Arabia!" . . . And definitely not starring MSNBC. It has no idea what you're talking about.

NOTES

1   "Yemen: U.S.-Backed Saudi Coalition Bombs Doctors Without Borders Cholera Clinic," Democracy Now! June 12, 2018, accessed September 24, 2019, https://www.democracynow.org/2018/6/12/headlines/yemen_us_backed_saudi_coalition_bombs_doctors_without_borders_cholera_clinic.

2   ACTION ALERT: It's Been Over a Year Since MSNBC Has Mentioned US War in Yemen," FAIR, July 23, 2018, accessed September 24, 2019, https://fair.org/home/action-alert-its-been-over-a-year-since-msnbc-has-mentioned-us-war-in-yemen/.

3   Peter Koenig, "What Really Happens to Nicaragua, Venezuela and Ecuador," MintPress News, August 14, 2018, accessed September 24, 2019, https://www.mintpressnews.com/really-happens-nicaragua-venezuela-ecuador/247643/.

4   "Key Neocon Calls on US to Oust Putin," Consortium News, October 7, 2016, accessed September 24, 2019, https://consortiumnews.com/2016/10/07/key-neocon-calls-on-us-to-oust-putin/.

5   "US Imposes Sanctions against Venezuela's Petro Cryptocurrency," MintPress News, March 19, 2018, accessed September 24, 2019, https://www.mintpressnews.com/us-imposes-sanctions-venezuelas-petro-cryptocurrency/239170/.

6   Koenig, "What Really Happens to Nicaragua, Venezuela and Ecuador."

7   Benjamin Waddell, "Laying the Groundwork for Insurrection: A Closer Look at the U.S. Role in Nicaragua's Social Unrest," Global Americans, May 1, 2018, accessed September 24, 2019, https://theglobalamericans.org/2018/05/laying-groundwork-insurrection-closer-look-u-s-role-nicaraguas-social-unrest/.

8   "US Gov't Regime Change Machine Exacerbates Nicaragua's Violent Protests," Real News Network, June 23, 2018, accessed September 24, 2019, https://therealnews.com/stories/us-govt-regime-change-machine-fuels-nicaraguas-violent-right-wing-insurgency.

9   Ramona Wadi, "The School of the Americas Is Still Exporting Death Squads," MintPress News, April 22, 2015, accessed September 24, 2019, https://www.mintpressnews.com/the-school-of-the-americas-is-still-exporting-death-squads/204655/.

10   "Exclusive Breaking News: President Aristide Says 'I Was Kidnapped' 'Tell the World It Is a Coup,'" Democracy Now! March 1, 2004, accessed September 24, 2019, https://www.democracynow.org/2004/3/1/exclusive_breaking_news_br_president_aristide.

11   "'Economic Hit Man' John Perkins Recounts US Efforts to Block Nationalization of Panama Canal," Democracy Now! May 8, 2008, accessed September 24, 2019, https://www.democracynow.org/2008/5/8/economic_hit_man_john_perkins_recounts.

12   Alexander Smith, "Fidel Castro: The CIA's 7 Most Bizarre Assassination Attempts," NBC News, November 28, 2016, accessed September 24, 2019, https://www.nbcnews.com/storyline/fidel-castros-death/fidel-castro-cia-s-7-most-bizarre-assassination-attempts-n688951.

13   "CIA Documents Show Bush Knew of 2002 Coup in Venezuela," Democracy Now! November 29, 2004, accessed September 24, 2019, https://www.democracynow.org/2004/11/29/cia_documents_show_bush_knew_of.

THE PENTAGON FAILED ITS FIRST-EVER AUDIT AMID A 21 TRILLION DOLLAR SCANDAL

New York Congresswoman-elect Alexandria Ocasio-Cortez was ruthlessly attacked recently, and I feel a bit responsible. I might have accidentally tainted her Twitter feed with truth serum.

But that sounds weird—so let me back up.

A few months ago, I covered the story of the 21 trillion dollars that has gone unaccounted for at the Pentagon.[1] That's right—trillion with a "T"—an amount of money you can't possibly come to terms with, so stop trying. Seriously, stop.

The 21 trillion dollars includes 6.5 trillion dollars unaccounted for at the Pentagon in 2015 *alone*. When I covered all this a few months ago, very few people were talking about it. David DeGraw investigated it for his website (which has since been destroyed by hackers), and Mark Skidmore, the economist who discovered the unaccounted for adjustments, coauthored a single *Forbes* article on the subject.[2] And by "discovered," I don't mean that Skidmore found a dusty shoebox in Donald Rumsfeld's desk underneath the standard pile of baby skeletons. I mean that he took a minute to look at the Defense Department's *own* inspector general's report. So, really, he just bothered to look at the thing that was designed for the public to look at.

Anyway, my column on this topic went viral, as did the *Forbes* article, each garnering hundreds of thousands of views.

Despite all that, still not a word from Congress or from the hacks at your mainstream media outlets. Then again, getting important news about the corruption of our military-industrial complex from the mainstream media would be like getting a philosophy lesson from a strip club dancer (in that it would be most unexpected, and it's not really why you're there).

But just a few weeks ago, something significant happened. It took place in a quiet news dump during a Pentagon press conference that truly began like this:

> DEPUTY SECRETARY OF DEFENSE PATRICK SHANAHAN: So you guys know why I came down here today?
> REPORTER: To see if we ate the donuts?[3]

Yes, Pentagon press conferences apparently begin in much the same manner as a sketch from The Three Stooges. (Unfortunately, the subsequent bonks on the head usually involve Tomahawk missiles.)

Halfway through that wacky press conference, the deputy secretary of defense casually mentioned that the Pentagon had failed its first-ever audit.[4] This is the first time the Pentagon has *ever* been audited, even though it has been legally required to do so since the early 1990s. Don't you wish *you* could put off your tax returns for 20 years? (I once put them off for two years, but it wasn't a conscious decision. It was simply the period of my life when I discovered that Netflix had every episode of The West Wing.)

After Shanahan dropped this bombshell, here was what followed:

> REPORTER: What part did the Pentagon fail in the audit?
> SHANAHAN: How about I give you, like, the technical version of that—there are a considerable number of areas where we kind of had a pass, then there's some other ones where they went through and they said we

went into your inventory system and we didn't find
these things; therefore that's a finding, so you don't
have a clean assessment. So—and—in a lot of these
audits, it's the type of finding that matters.[5]

Yes, the Pentagon's official response to why it failed its
audit is a word salad after it has gone through an industrial-
grade militarized Slap Chop. It's the type of response you
get when a fraud has been filtered through a cover-up, then
filtered through a publicist, then filtered through a public
official who probably doesn't know that much to begin with.

It's the corrupt feeding the blind feeding the stupid
feeding the disingenuous.

Yet even *that* didn't get much press coverage. As far as I
can tell, the *New York Times* didn't report on the audit failure
until two weeks later, and even that column contained this
caveat: "But audits are hard work; most defense officials
aren't business experts; and to some, bookkeeping and other
management operations just aren't a priority in wartime,
which since Sept. 11, 2001, has been a permanent state."[6]

In the *Times'* defense, there are different genres of reporting, and in this case, journalists were working in the genre of
"shit reporting." Should we really be surprised? If they want to
learn what real reporting looks like on this same topic, they
can read the *Nation's* investigative exposé. That article stated:

> For decades, the DoD's leaders and accountants
> have been perpetrating a gigantic, unconstitutional
> accounting fraud, deliberately cooking the books to
> mislead the Congress and drive the DoD's budgets ever
> higher. . . . DoD has literally been making up numbers
> in its annual financial reports to Congress—represent-
> ing trillions of dollars' worth of seemingly nonexistent
> transactions . . . according to government records and
> interviews with current and former DoD officials, con-
> gressional sources, and independent experts.[7]

It doesn't get much clearer than that. (The following page in the magazine was simply an image of a hand dropping a mic.)

So here's how this fraud works: every year, the Pentagon tells Congress how much money it needs. It submits the financial reports from the year before, filled to the brim with heaping, steaming bullshit. Trillions of gallons of bullshit, called "adjustments." Those adjustments cover up the fact that it didn't necessarily spend all the money the year before.

"However, instead of returning such unspent funds to the US Treasury, as the law requires, the Pentagon sometimes launders and shifts such moneys to other parts of the DoD's budget," the Nation's Dave Lindorff wrote.

And this is no mistake. This is straight-up fraud. How do you know when something is fraud? Well, one way is when the paper trail is covered up. As Lindorff noted: "Indeed, more than 16,000 records that might reveal either the source or the destination of some of that $6.5 trillion had been 'removed,' the inspector general's office reported."

Sixteen *thousand* records! By my calculations, such a cover-up would require multiple shredder operators working in shifts, only stopping once every five hours to use the bathroom and briefly giggle at their villainy.

> One congressional staffer [said], "We don't know how the Pentagon's money is being spent. . . . We don't know how much of that funding gets spent on the intended programs, what things actually cost, whether payments are going to the proper accounts. If this kind of stuff were happening in the private sector, people would be fired and prosecuted."[8]

Here's more analysis from the Nation:

> The Pentagon's accounting fraud diverts many billions of dollars that could be devoted to other national needs: health care, education, job creation, climate action, infrastructure modernization, and more.

Indeed, the Pentagon's accounting fraud amounts to theft on a grand scale—theft not only from America's taxpayers, but also from the nation's well-being and its future.

Apparently, disappearing at least 16 thousand documents wasn't enough. Somebody might still connect the dots. So the Pentagon took the next step:

> [T]he most recent report for the DOD on the OIG website . . . summarizes unsupported adjustments for fiscal year 2017. However, this document differs from all previous reports in that all the numbers relating to the unsupported adjustments were redacted. That is, all the relevant information was blacked out.[9]

Right after the *Nation* article came out, Ocasio-Cortez tweeted about it—basically saying that these unaccounted trillions at the Pentagon could help pay for "Medicare for all" (@AOC, December 2, 2018).

Clearly things are ramping up. People are finding out about the 21 trillion dollars, and that means it is now time for the true hacks—the military-industrial complex defenders—to jump in and chastise anyone who dares speak out about this fraud. Enter Vox—which, if you're unfamiliar, is a cross between HuffPost and an NPR tote bag filled with rotting raccoon carcasses.

Vox ran an article titled, "The $21 trillion accounting error that can't pay for Medicare-for-all, explained."[10] You know how to tell for sure that you're a nitwit spraying idiocy like a Super Soaker? When you find yourself saying the phrase "21 trillion dollar accounting error."

Error?! Yeah, and Timothy McVeigh just had a faulty carburetor.

Vox "journalist" Matthew Yglesias tried to push this idiotic justification: "The Pentagon's accounting errors are genuinely enormous, but they're also just accounting errors—they don't represent actual money that can be spent on something else."

Sorry, but no. These are not "accounting errors." It's impossible to have trillions of dollars of "accounting errors." Since I have now saturated my keyboard with my anger saliva, I'll let Laurence Kotlikoff at *Forbes* answer this:

> Let's recall that this is not simply a matter of boring accounting. Trillions in unaccounted outlays, if that's what's involved here, is trillions of our tax dollars being spent without our knowledge. If that's the case, we're talking about the biggest government financial deception in the history of the country.[11]

Long story short, this 21 trillion dollar story is starting to gain traction. People can finally see the truth. And, right now, it is the corporate media puppets who are trying to make sure you think, "It's just a few accounting errors. Pay no mind to the fact that it amounts to the largest theft ever perpetrated against the American people."

NOTES

1   See "The Pentagon Can't Account for 21 Trillion Dollars (That's Not a Typo)," in this volume.

2   Laurence Kotlikoff, "Has Our Government Spent $21 Trillion of Our Money without Telling Us?," *Forbes*, December 8, 2017, accessed September 24, 2019, https://www.forbes.com/sites/kotlikoff/2017/12/08/has-our-government-spent-21-trillion-of-our-money-without-telling-us/#5f2213917aef.

3   U.S. Department of Defense, "Press Gaggle by Deputy Secretary," November 15, 2018, accessed September 24, 2019, https://www.defense.gov/Newsroom/Transcripts/Transcript/Article/1692090/press-gaggle-by-deputy-secretary-shanahan/.

4   Bill Chappell, "Pentagon Announces First-Ever Audit of the Department of Defense," NPR, December 8, 2017, accessed September 24, 2019, https://www.npr.org/sections/thetwo-way/2017/12/08/569394885/pentagon-announces-first-ever-audit-of-the-department-of-defense.

5   U.S. Department of Defense, "Press Gaggle by Deputy Secretary."

6   "The Pentagon Doesn't Know Where Its Money Goes," *New York Times*, December 1, 2018, accessed September 24, 2019, https://www.nytimes.com/2018/12/01/opinion/sunday/pentagon-spending-audit-failed.html.

7   Dave Lindorff, "The Pentagon's Massive Accounting Fraud Exposed," *Nation*, January 7, 2019, accessed September 24, 2019, https://www.thenation.com/article/pentagon-audit-budget-fraud/.

8   Ibid.

9   Laurence Kotlikoff, "Is Our Government Intentionally Hiding $21 Trillion in Spending?" *Forbes*, July 21, 2018, accessed September 24, 2019, https://www.forbes.com/sites/kotlikoff/2018/07/21/is-our-government-intentionally-hiding-21-trillion-in-spending/#2b9a00ca4a73.

10   Matthew Yglesias, "The $21 Trillion Pentagon Accounting Error That Can't Pay for Medicare-for-All, Explained," Vox, December 3, 2018, accessed September 24, 2019, https://www.vox.com/policy-and-politics/2018/12/3/18122947/pentagon-accounting-error-medicare-for-all.

11   Kotlikoff, "Is Our Government Intentionally Hiding $21 Trillion in Spending?"

THE TOP FOUR TIMES AMERICANS HAVE BEEN LIED INTO WAR

I was 22 when we invaded Iraq, and I wasn't sure it was based on lies, but something deep down in me—just behind the spleen—told me it was based on lies. Kinda like if your blind date shows up and you notice he has a 2004 flip phone. It seems vaguely worrisome, and no explanation he can haltingly supply will put you at ease. Plus, anyone else who acts like it's normal also becomes suspect.

The invasion of Iraq just felt like it was a lie to me. And it turned out that I was right, that it was a lie, and that the entirety of the mainstream media and our government were either wrong or lying and, most of the time, both.

Now our government and our media are trying their damnedest to lie us into another war, this one with Venezuela. They tell us the Venezuelan people are desperate for necessities like toothpaste, while independent journalists show piles of affordable toothpaste in Caracas.[1]

And even if they didn't have toothpaste, that hardly seems like a good reason for America to begin dropping our long-range bad decisions on the heads of innocent people. Turning a town into an impact crater for the sake of a battle to stop gingivitis seems a bit extreme.

The mainstream media and nearly the entirety of the US government tell us Juan Guaidó is the "interim president," even though he was never elected to that position and the current president is still leading the Venezuelan government and military. So I guess this "interim" is the time between Guaidó being a nobody and the time when he goes back to being nobody but gets to tell women at parties, "You know, I used to be interim president."

The mainstream media also inform us that the Venezuelan military set US aid trucks on fire, when video shows opposition forces doing it.[2] Furthermore, the idea of Venezuela taking "aid" from the country whose sanctions are crushing them would be like the Standing Rock Sioux accepting gift packages from the construction crews swiss cheesing their land to lay down the Dakota Access pipeline. Unless the boxes are filled with industrial paper towels to help clean up oil spills, I fail to see how it would be beneficial. Sometimes you do indeed have to look a gift horse in the mouth (or should I say "gift dog").[3]

This is not the first time our government and our media have conspired to drag the American people into war with another country—or helped create a coup that will inevitably have disastrous results. So I thought this would be a prime moment to go through the top four greatest hits.

Number 4: The Spanish-American War

This is widely considered to be the birth of modern media propaganda, because it was the first war actually started by the media.[4] Newspapers fabricated atrocities in the never-ending quest for more readers.

And as the *New York Times* noted:

> [T]he sensationalistic reporting of the sinking of the American battleship Maine in Havana harbor on Feb. 15, 1898 . . . and all the other egregious reporting leading up to the Spanish-American War might have been considered merely cartoonish if it hadn't led to a major international conflict.[5]

I think maybe the *New York Times* got that quote confused with its mission statement: "Cartoonishly dragging America into major international conflicts since 1851!"

Number 3: The Vietnam War

Sure, most everyone knows the catastrophic Vietnam War was precipitated by the Gulf of Tonkin incident, in which US naval vessels were fired upon by villainous North Vietnamese torpedo boats. Following that skirmish, Defense Secretary Robert McNamara recommended that President Johnson retaliate, and the full-force Vietnam War began. But most Americans still don't know that there was no Gulf of Tonkin incident—unless you count US naval ships literally firing their weapons at weather events they saw on the radar. The 2003 documentary *The Fog of War* finally revealed the truth. Former Secretary of Defense Robert McNamara confessed that the Gulf of Tonkin attack did not actually happen.[6]

That's right. It never happened. Much like leprechauns or dragons or Simon Cowell's talent, it was a figment of our national imagination.

The lies of our government, followed by the fawning, credulous reporting from our media, led to the death of 58 thousand US service members and as many as 3.8 million Vietnamese.

The United States government has one of the most powerful Departments of Fabrication and Falsification ever assembled. It's a modern marvel on par with the Great Pyramid of Giza and Rafael Nadal's down-the-line running forehand.

Number 2: The Iraq War

Of course, there's the most obvious lie about Iraq—that Saddam Hussein had so many weapons of mass destruction, that he would often use one to scrub hard to reach places while in the tub. But that wasn't the only falsehood manifested to bring about our complete annihilation of the sovereign nation Saddam ruled over. There were others, such as the idea that Saddam was connected to al-Qaida and perhaps played a role in the 9/11 attacks. In May 2002, William Safire at the *New York Times* wrote, "Mohamed Atta, destined to be the leading Sept. 11 suicide hijacker, was reported last fall by Czech intelligence to have met at least once with Saddam Hussein's espionage chief in the Iraqi Embassy."[7]

Yes, Safire was able to polish a load of bullshit so thoroughly it would sparkle like a sapphire. And that column is still up on the *Times* website, without a correction or retraction. I would say the *Times* is only useful for covering the bottom of a birdcage, but I'd fear the paper would lie your pet cockatoo into an ill-advised invasion, killing millions.

But the propaganda didn't stop there. There were also the anthrax attacks following 9/11. Anthrax was mailed to press outlets and the offices of politicians. To this day, many people still believe it had something to do with Iraq or al-Qaida because of award-winning national embarrassments like Brian Ross.[8]

"Brian Ross at ABC News wrote 'the anthrax in the tainted letter sent to Senate Majority Leader Tom Daschle was laced with bentonite' and 'bentonite is a trademark of Iraqi leader Saddam Hussein's biological weapons program.'" As Salon so clearly put it, "All of those factual claims . . . were completely false, demonstrably and unquestionably so. . . . Yet neither ABC nor Ross have ever retracted, corrected, clarified, or explained these fraudulent reports."

And, as you would expect, following that blatantly false reporting, Brian Ross did not lose his job. In fact, he wasn't put out to pasture from ABC News until last year, when he "reported that fired national security adviser Michael Flynn was ready to testify that Trump told him to contact the Russians during the campaign."[9]

That report—much like the rumors of Brian Ross's journalistic integrity—turned out to be absolutely false.

(In my professional opinion, anyone who had anything to do with the selling, perpetrating, or planning of the Iraq

War should never again hold a position higher than assistant trainee to the guy who picks up the shit of a dog that does not belong to anyone of any particular importance. If that position does not exist, we as a nation should create it just for this moment. Yet, despite my objections, Robert Mueller (head of the FBI at the time of the invasion and a big supporter of it) is leading the biggest investigation in the country. John Bolton, who advocated for the Iraq invasion as far back as the 1990s, is now national security adviser. Bill Kristol, who pushed for the war and said it would last two months, is now a regular panelist on MSNBC. And the list goes on.)

Unlike Defense Secretary McNamara, who admitted the Gulf of Tonkin incident never happened, we don't have a smoking gun showing that the Bush administration created these lies to get us into Iraq. . . . Oh, wait! Turns out the paper shredder at the Bush Oval Office was on strike for a higher minimum wage in 2002, and, in fact, we *do* have a memo written by Bush's defense secretary Donald Rumsfeld a year *before* US forces unleashed a reign of terror on the Iraqi people. His memo about war with Iraq stated, "How start? US discovers Saddam connection to Sept 11 or to anthrax attacks? Or maybe a dispute over WMD inspections?"[10]

I'm not sure what's more striking—that this memo exists or that it sounds like the Bush boys planned a massive international battle the same way a broke 35-year-old maps out his bad novel that he's sure is the ticket out of his mom's basement.

"How start horrible bloody war? Maybe Saddam found to moonlight as porn star?"

Point is, multiple completely false stories laid the groundwork for an invasion of Iraq that left well over one million people dead.[11]

Number 1: The Bombing of Syria
President Bashar Assad gassed his own people, thereby guaranteeing more American involvement—and he did it

just days after Donald Trump had told the Pentagon to begin withdrawing troops from Syria. At least, that's the story the corporate media repeated on loop for more than a month, only pausing every 10 minutes to try desperately to get us all to buy more things with "Baconator" in the name or to seek out a harder penis.

So we are expected to believe Assad did the one thing that would ensure more US involvement just as he was about to win his war? It's kinda like how, when I'm about to win a fistfight, I often poke myself repeatedly in the eye. You know—just to keep it exciting.

Famed journalists Seymour Hersh and Robert Fisk have done great work showing that the chemical attacks never happened, but there's a new update.[12] Just two weeks ago, a BBC producer came forward and said the Douma, Syria, chemical attack footage was staged.[13]

His tweet said that after six months of investigation, he can prove that no fatalities occurred in the hospital. Yet our breathlessly inept mainstream American media, with little to no evidence, ran around saying, "There was a chemical attack! Those poor people! And they don't have toothpaste either! We must bomb them to help them!"

The overarching point here is that we replaced our media with stenographers to the ruling elite long ago. The ruling class comes up with a lie to manufacture American consent for its all-American war crimes, and that lie is then sprayed like laminate all over average American citizens. This goes on until such time as any average citizens who question said lie are looked at like they have two heads—and one of them is covered in rat shit.

For the "journalists" who hose the lies across the country the best, awards and private jets and rooftop drinks with midlevel celebrities like Chuck Norris await them. Now we're getting to the point where the actual rulers—the Trump administration, etc.—are not even hiding their corruption. John Bolton stated on Fox News that the ultimate goal is to steal Venezuela's oil.[14] But our media continue to tout the propaganda line. Even after Bolton said that, you won't see Anderson Cooper or one of the Fox News grand wizards saying, "Venezuela is undergoing a US-backed coup, because we'd like to steal their oil." It's truly dizzying that the corporate media preserve the propaganda even after the "leaders" have revealed their true sinister intentions.

On the inside of Wolf Blitzer's eyelids the phrase "Must Defend the Matrix" blinks in red.

The propaganda line for Venezuela right now is: "We want to help the poor Venezuelans." Well, if you want to help them, then keep America out of their face. Don't force them to have anything to do with the country that came up with drive-through fried food served in a bucket and opioid nasal sprays. At no point does anyone look at the Donald Trump presidency and think, "Wow, that country really has things figured out. I hope they bring some of their great decision-making to our doorstep."

NOTES

1   Grayzone, "The Real Humanitarian Aid: Inside Venezuela's State-Subsidized Communal Markets," YouTube, February 24, 2019, accessed September 24, 2019, https://www.youtube.com/watch?time_continue=29&v=qlX3yfXNX_g.

2   Max Blumenthal, "Burning Aid: An Interventionist Deception on Colombia-Venezuela Bridge?" Grayzone, February 24, 2019, accessed September 24, 2019, https://grayzoneproject.com/2019/02/24/burning-aid-colombia-venezuela-bridge/.

3   "Dakota Access Pipeline Company Attacks Native American Protesters with Dogs and Pepper Spray," Democracy Now! September 4, 2016, accessed September 24, 2019, https://www.democracynow.org/2016/9/4/dakota_access_pipeline_company_attacks_native.

4   George W. Auxier, "Middle Western Newspapers and the Spanish-American War, 1895–1898," *Journal of American History* 26, no. 4 (March 1940): 523–34, accessed September 24, 2019, https://academic.oup.com/jah/article-abstract/26/4/523/786716.

5   Clifford Krauss, "The World; Remember Yellow Journalism," *New York Times*, February 15, 1998, accessed September 24, 2019, https://www.

nytimes.com/1998/02/15/weekinreview/the-world-remember-yellow-journalism.html.

6　Compelled2283, "Gulf of Tonkin: McNamara Admits It Didn't Happen," YouTube, March 4, 2008, accessed September 25, 2019, https://youtu.be/HODxnUrFX6k?t=130.

7　William Safire, "Mr. Atta Goes to Prague," *New York Times*, May 9, 2002, accessed September 25, 2019, https://www.nytimes.com/2002/05/09/opinion/mr-atta-goes-to-prague.html?mtrref=duckduckgo.com.

8　Glenn Greenwald, "The Unresolved Story of ABC News' False Saddam-Anthrax Reports," Salon, April 9, 2007, accessed September 25, 2019, https://www.salon.com/2007/04/09/abc_anthrax/.

9　Erik Wemple, "Brian Ross's Career at ABC News Comes to a Quiet End," *Washington Post*, July 2, 2018, accessed September 25, 2019, https://www.washingtonpost.com/blogs/erik-wemple/wp/2018/07/02/brian-rosss-career-at-abc-news-comes-to-a-quiet-end/?utm_term=.14a98cf6273a.

10　"Newly-Released Memo by Donald Rumsfeld Proves Iraq War Started on False Pretenses," Washington's Blog, February 20, 2013, accessed September 25, 2019, https://washingtonsblog.com/2013/02/newly-released-memos-of-donald-rumsfeld-prove-knowing-iraq-war.html.

11　Medea Benjamin, "The Iraq Death Toll 15 Years After the US Invasion," Common Dreams, March 15, 2018, accessed September 25, 2019, https://www.commondreams.org/views/2018/03/15/iraq-death-toll-15-years-after-us-invasion.

12　Seymour M. Hersh, "Trump's Red Line," *Welt*, June 25, 2017, accessed September 25, 2019, https://www.welt.de/politik/ausland/article165905578/Trump-s-Red-Line.htm; Robert Fisk, "The Search for Truth in the Rubble of Douma—and One Doctor's Doubts over the Chemical Attack," *Independent*, April 17, 2018, accessed September 25, 2019, https://www.independent.co.uk/voices/syria-chemical-attack-gas-douma-robert-fisk-ghouta-damascus-a8307726.html.

13　ZeroHedge.com, "BBC Producer Says Syria Douma Chemical Attack Footage 'Was Staged,'" MintPress News, February 15, 2019, accessed September 25, 2019, https://www.mintpressnews.com/bbc-producer-says-syria-douma-chemical-attack-footage-was-staged/255152/.

14　Karoli Kuns, "John Bolton Says Ultimate Goal in Venezuela Is to Take Their Oil," Crooks and Liars, January 26, 2019, accessed September 25, 2019, https://crooksandliars.com/2019/01/john-bolton-says-ultimate-goal-venezuela.

I KNOW WHICH COUNTRY THE US WILL INVADE NEXT

Dear reader, the following column was first published months before my prediction was proven completely correct. Okay, I should've changed the word "invade" in the title to "try desperately to destroy," but you get the point. I was—and am always—right. Just sayin'. . .

By the end of this column, it will be clear which country the US will invade and topple next. . . . Or—failing that—it will be clear which country our military intelligence industrial complex will be *aching* to invade next.

We all want to know why America does what it does. And I don't mean why *Americans* do what we do. I think that question will still be pondered eons from now by a future professor showing his students a video-mind-meld of present-day UFC fighters booting each other in the head while thrilled onlookers cheer (not for either of the fighters but, rather, for more booting in the head).

But we all seem to assume that America—the entity, the corporation—has some sort of larger reasoning behind the actions it takes, the actions put forward by the ruling elite. And almost all of us know the reasons we're given by the press secretaries and caricature-shaped heads on the nightly news are the ripest, most fetid grade of bullshit.

We now know the invasion of Iraq had literally nothing to do with weapons of mass destruction. We now know crushing Libya had nothing to do with "stopping a bad man." If one does even a cursory check of what dictators around the world are up to recently, you'll find the US doesn't care in the slightest whether they are bad or good, whether they're using their free time to kill thousands of innocent people or to harmonize their rock garden. In fact, the US gives military aid to 70 percent of the world's dictators.[1] (One would hope that's only around the holidays though.)

So if it's not for the stated reasons, then why does the US overrun, topple, and sometimes occupy the countries it does. Obviously, there are oil resources or rare earth minerals to be had. But there's something else that links almost all of our recent wars.

As the *Guardian* reported near the beginning of the Iraq War, "In October 2000, Iraq insisted on dumping the US dollar—the currency of the enemy—for the more multilateral euro."[2]

However, one example does not make a trend. If it did I would be a world-renowned beer pong champion rather than touting a 1–27 record. (I certainly can't go pro with those numbers.)

But there's more. Soon after Libya began moving toward an African gold-based currency—and lining up all their African neighbors to join them—we invaded them as well—with the help of NATO. Author Ellen Brown pointed out this fact at the time of the invasion: "Gaddafi initiated a movement to refuse the dollar and the euro, and called on Arab and African nations to use a new currency instead, the gold dinar."[3] John Perkins, author of *Confessions of an Economic Hitman*, also said that the true reason for the attack on Libya was Gaddafi's move away from the dollar and the euro.[4]

This week, the Intercept reported that the ousting of Gaddafi, which was in many ways led by President Sarkozy of France, actually had to do with Sarkozy secretly receiving millions from Gaddafi, and it seemed his corruption was about to be revealed.[5] But the article also noted, "[Sarkozy's] real military zeal and desire for regime change came only after Clinton and the Arab League broadcasted their desire to see Gaddafi go." And the fact that Gaddafi was planning to upend the petrodollar in Africa certainly provides the motivation necessary. (It doesn't take much to get the US excited about a new bombing campaign. I'm pretty sure we invaded Madagascar once in the 1970s, because they smoked our good weed.)

Right now, you may be thinking, "But, Lee, your theory is ridiculous. If these invasions were about the banking, then the rebels in Libya—getting help from NATO and the United States—would've set up a new banking system after bringing down Gaddafi!"

Actually, they didn't wait that long. In the middle of the brutal war, the Libyan rebels formed their own central bank.[6] Ellen Brown wrote, "Several writers have noted the odd fact that the Libyan rebels took time out from their rebellion in March to create their own central bank—this before they even had a government."[7]

Wow, that sure does sound like it's all about the banking!

Many of you know about General Wesley Clark's famous quote about seven countries in five years. Clark is a four-star general, the former head of NATO Supreme Allied Command, and he ran for president in 2008. (Clearly, he's an underachiever.) But it's quite possible that 100 years from now, the one thing he'll be remembered for is the fact that he told us the Pentagon said to him in 2002, "We're going to take down seven countries in five years. We're going to start with Iraq, then Syria, Lebanon, then Libya, Somalia, Sudan, we're going to come back and get Iran in five years."[8]

Most of those have happened. We've, of course, added some to the list, like Yemen. We're helping to destroy Yemen largely to make Saudi Arabia happy. Apparently, our government/media only care about Syrian children (to justify regime change). We couldn't care less about Yemeni children, Iraqi children, Afghan children, Palestinian children, North

Korean children, Somalian children, Flint, Michigan, children, Baltimore children, Native American children, Puerto Rican children, Na'vi children. . . . Oh, wait, I think that's from *Avatar*. Was that fiction? My memories and 3D movies are starting to blur together.

Ellen Brown goes even further in her analysis of General Clark's bombshell:

> What do these seven countries have in common? . . .
> None of them is listed among the 56 member banks
> of the Bank for International Settlements (BIS). That
> evidently puts them outside the long regulatory arm of
> the central bankers' central bank in Switzerland. The
> most renegade of the lot could be Libya and Iraq, the
> two that have actually been attacked.[9]

What I'm trying to say is—it's all about *the banking*!

So, right now you're thinking, "But, Lee, then why is the US so eager to turn Syria into a failed state, if Syria never dropped the dollar? Your whole stupid theory falls apart right there!"

First, I don't appreciate your tone. Second, in February 2006, Syria dropped the dollar as their primary hard currency.[10]

I think I'm noticing a trend. In fact, on January 4, 2018, it was reported that Pakistan was ditching the dollar in its trade with China,[11] and that *same day* the US placed them on the watch list for religious freedom violations.[12] The same day? Are we really supposed to believe that it just so happened Pakistan stopped using the dollar with China on the same day they started punching Christians in the nose for no good reason? No, clearly Pakistan had violated our religion of cold hard cash.

This leaves only one question: Who is next on the list of US illegal invasions cloaked in bullshit justifications? . . . Well, last week, Iran finally did it: they switched from the dollar to the euro. And sure enough, this week the US military-industrial complex, the corporate media, and Israel all got together to claim Iran is lying about their nuclear weapons development.[13] What are the odds this news would break within *days* of Iran dropping the dollar? What . . . are . . . the . . . odds?

The one nice thing about our corporate state's manufacturing of consent is how predictable it is. We will now see the mainstream media running an increasing number of reports claiming Iran is a sponsor of terrorism and is trying to develop nuclear weapons (which are WMD, but for some strange reason our media are shying away from the sentence: "They have WMD"). A recent State Department report claims that Iran is the top state sponsor of terrorism.[14] One must assume this list of terror sponsors does not include the country that made the arms that significantly enhanced ISIS's military capabilities.[15] (It's the US.)

Or the country that drops hundreds of bombs *per day* on the Middle East.[16] (It's the US.) But those bombs don't cause any terror. Those are clearly the happy bombs. Apparently, we just drop 1995 Richard Simmons down on unsuspecting people.

Point is, as you watch our pathetic corporate media continue their manufacturing of consent for war with Iran, don't fall for it. These wars are all about the banking. And millions of innocent people are killed in them. Millions more have their lives destroyed.

You and I are just pawns in this game, and the last thing the ruling elite want is pawns that question the official narrative.

NOTES

1   The Free Thought Project, "'Promoting Democracy'? US Gives Military Aid to More than 70% of World's Dictatorships," September 26, 2017, accessed September 25, 2019, https://thefreethoughtproject.com/democracy-us-funding-dictatorships/.

2   Faisal Islam, "Iraq Nets Handsome Profit by Dumping Dollar for Euro," *Guardian*, February 15, 2003, accessed September 25, 2019, https://www.theguardian.com/business/2003/feb/16/iraq.theeuro.

3   Ellen Brown, "Libya: All about Oil, or All about Banking?," Web of Debt Blog, April 16, 2011, accessed September 25, 2019, https://ellenbrown.com/2011/04/16/libya-all-about-oil-or-all-about-banking/.

4   John Perkins, *Confessions of an Economic Hitman* (San Francisco: Berrett-Koehler Publishers, 2004).

5   Joe Penney, "Why Did the U.S. and Its Allies Bomb Libya? Corruption Case against Sarkozy Sheds New Light on Ousting of Gaddafi," Intercept, April 28, 2018, accessed September 25, 2019, https://theintercept.com/2018/04/28/sarkozy-gaddafi-libya-bombing/.

6   John Carney, "Libyan Rebels Form Their Own Central Bank," CNBC, March 28, 2011, accessed September 25, 2019, https://www.cnbc.com/id/42308613.

7   Brown, "Libya."

8   "General Wesley Clark: Wars Were Planned—Seven Countries in Five Years," YouTube, September 11, 2011, accessed September 25, 2019, https://www.youtube.com/watch?v=9RC1Mepk_Sw; originally aired on *Democracy Now!* March 2007.

9   Brown, "Libya."

10 "Syria Dollar Dropped as Primary Hard Currency," *Chicago Tribune*, February 15, 2006, accessed September 25, 2019, https://www.chicagotribune.com/news/ct-xpm-2006-02-15-0602150153-story.html.

11 "Pakistan Is Ditching the Dollar for Trade with China" (video), CNBC, January 4, 2018, accessed September 25, 2019, https://www.cnbc.com/video/2018/01/04/pakistan-is-ditching-the-dollar-for-trade-with-china--24-hours-after-trump-denounced-the-country.html.

12 "U.S. Placed Pakistan on Watch List for Religious Freedom Violations," Reuters, January 4, 2018, accessed September 25, 2019, https://reut.rs/2mv87qt.

13 "Iran Switches from Dollar to Euro," Middle East Monitor, April 19, 2018, accessed September 25, 2019, https://www.middleeastmonitor.com/20180419-iran-switches-from-dollar-to-euro/.

14 Michael Lee, "Iran Still Top State Sponsor of Terrorism, U.S. Report Says," PBS, July 19, 2017, accessed September 25, 2019, https://www.pbs.org/newshour/world/iran-still-top-state-sponsor-terrorism-u-s-report-says.

15 Bethan McKernan, "US and Saudi Arabia Arms Significantly Enhanced Isis' Military Capabilities, Report Reveals," *Independent*, December 15, 2017, accessed September 25, 2019, https://www.independent.co.uk/news/world/middle-east/isis-us-saudi-arabia-arms-fighters-

jihadis-military-capability-enhanced-weapons-syria-terrorism-a8112076.html.

16   John Haltiwanger, "Trump Has Dropped Record Number of Bombs on Middle East," *Newsweek*, September 19, 2017, accessed September 25, 2019, https://www.newsweek.com/trump-era-record-number-bombs-dropped-middle-east-667505.

NEARLY 100 THOUSAND PENTAGON WHISTLEBLOWER COMPLAINTS HAVE BEEN SILENCED

I don't know if I'd have the nerve to be a whistleblower. I'd like to think I would. We all like to think we would, just like we all like to think we could catch the game-winning touchdown, triumph on "America's Got Talent," and fold a fitted sheet quickly without cursing.

But to blow the whistle on a huge organization with a lot of power, likely bringing that power crashing down on your head—that takes some serious spine-age. Now, imagine the organization you're calling out is arguably the largest, most powerful, most secretive, and most violent organization on planet Earth. I'm speaking, of course, of the U.S. Department of Defense.

Yet thousands, even tens of thousands, of people have taken that step over the past five years. (More on this in a moment.)

All the while our organized human murder machine continues its work around the world. Every day. Every hour. Never a moment of rest. Never pausing to clip its toenails or scratch its ass. Bombs dropped. Buildings blown up. People killed or imprisoned. No end in sight.

By the way, that's the term I like to use instead of "military"—Organized Human Murder Machine.

It has a nice ring to it, doesn't it? "Military" sounds too boring, too banal. Sounds like a super-lame couple you met at a party. "Yeah, Millie and Terry over there are accountants. If I have to hear one more joke about capital gains taxes, I'm gonna kill myself."

But that's not what the military is. The military is a gigantic organized human murder machine, and even if you "support" every action our military has ever taken, you can still acknowledge it's an organized human murder machine. (You would just bizarrely argue that all the murder has been just and sound and pure.)

Eleven months ago, I covered a story about 21 trillion dollars of unaccounted for adjustments at the Pentagon over the past 20 years.[1] Don't try to think about the number 21 trillion, because you'll pass out and hit your head on the desk. Remember, if your salary is 40 thousand dollars a year, to earn 21 trillion dollars would take you 525 million years. (At which point you can't even enjoy the new jet ski you just bought with all your money, because you're almost certainly a brain in a jar . . . though a nice embroidered jar that only the rich brains can afford.)

Over the past year, there has been a little more coverage of the utterly preposterous amount of money unaccounted for at our human murder machine. The Nation, Forbes, and Congresswoman Alexandria Ocasio-Cortez all covered it.[2] Then the white blood cells of the military-industrial complex kicked into action in order to destroy the "infection." The New York Times and Vox both claimed the unaccounted for 21 trillion dollars is merely the result of large-scale misdocumentation and, therefore, doesn't matter at all. Of course, the idea that tens of trillions of dollars of unaccountable adjustments don't matter and couldn't mask any fraud, abuse, or corruption is an assertion that makes Charlie Sheen's statement that he runs on tiger blood seem downright levelheaded.

Probably the best article to date on the 21 trillion dollars was written a few weeks ago by Matt Taibbi for Rolling Stone.[3]

Point is, even though most of the mainstream media won't get near this subject (or worse yet—actively attack those who do), the word is getting out: there is a giant sucking sound in the center of the Pentagon, and whatever's down there feeds on trillions of secretive dollars, then shits out incalculable death and destruction. (It's the Death Star if officials at the Death Star spent 10 thousand dollars on a toilet seat.)[4]

A month ago, the Government Accountability Office came out with a report showing the total number of whistleblower complaints over the past five years at the Department of Defense. It's nearly 100 thousand. Here's the only part of the report that references that number: "The Department of Defense Inspector General identified 8 substantiated violations of whistleblower confidentiality between fiscal years 2013 and 2018, representing approximately .01 percent of the 95,613 contacts handled by the Inspector General during that time."[5]

Ninety-five thousand, six hundred and thirteen whistleblower complaints over five years.

Sadly, the Government Accountability Office was trying to brag in that sentence. They were proudly stating, "We only breached the confidentiality of .01 percent of our 95 thousand whistleblower complaints. Aren't we heroes?!"

It's kind of like saying, "Of the 10 thousand dolphins I've killed, not a single one has accidentally been a human." The sane response is, "Well, I'm glad to hear that, but did you say you killed 10 *thousand dolphins?*"

To try to get the 95 thousand number to make a little more sense, that averages out to a whistleblower every six minutes of every weekday for five straight years. (That waiting room must be truly nuts. I bet all the good magazines were claimed eons ago.)

But maybe I'm looking at this all wrong. Perhaps the number 95,613 shouldn't be all that shocking, and I need to roll my tongue back up and store it back in my mouth. When you have 21 trillion dollars of unaccounted for adjustments, it means a seizure-inducing amount of money, parts, pieces, bombs, missiles, manpower, and devices are flying around with no accountability—likely creating loads of fraud, which would probably create loads of whistleblowers. Hence, maybe we all should have expected this number of whistleblowers rather than being shocked.

For example, there's the time in 2003 when the US flew 12 billion dollars in cash to Iraq and promptly lost track of it. As the *Guardian* makes clear, this was not an instance of hackers on a computer system stealing a bunch of ones and zeroes.[6] This was giant pallets of cash money vanishing without a trace. In fact, it was 281 million 100-dollar bills, weighing in at 363 tons. That's not really the type of thing you can just smuggle away in your sweatshirt while humming "She'll be comin' 'round the mountain."

Or here's another example journalist David DeGraw highlights from the Government Accountability Report: "according to a Department of Defense official, during an initial audit, the Army found 39 Blackhawk helicopters that had not been recorded in the property system. [819 million dollars in value] Similarly, the Air Force identified 478 buildings and structures at 12 installations that were not in the real property systems."[7]

The Army lost and then found 39 helicopters.

The Air Force lost and then found 478 buildings.

How does one lose a goddamn building? Unless you just had a bad breakup with David Copperfield, there's no explanation for losing a building. (Side note: it must suck divorcing David Copperfield. "Really, honey? You think you're gonna take the house? PAFOOMPF! *What* house?!")

Ya see, this madness stems from the fact that the Pentagon has a standard operating procedure of simply making up numbers to fill their books—which for normal human beings is termed "fraud." But in the case of the Pentagon, it's termed, "We get to make shit up because . . . ummm . . . national security."

Here's more from a 2013 Reuters article:

Linda Woodford spent the last 15 years of her career inserting phony numbers in the Department of

Defense's accounts . . . but many mystery numbers remained. For those, Woodford and her colleagues were told by superiors to take "unsubstantiated change actions"—in other words, enter false numbers, commonly called "plugs," to make the Navy's totals match the Treasury's.[8]

Have no fear, patriotic Americans, this is not "lying to the American people, stealing their money, and using it for war," this is just "unsubstantiated change actions." Try that on your next tax return. Put in 10 thousand dollars marked "unsubstantiated change actions." I'm sure they'll love that.

So let's sum this up, shall we? The Pentagon sucks up 55 percent of all the discretionary tax money we pay to our government (thanks to our bought-off Congress, who receive more Christmas cards from weapons contractors than they do from relatives). Those who work at the Pentagon have no idea where or how the money is spent. They make up many of the numbers resulting in tens of trillions of dollars of unaccounted for adjustments. They lose helicopters, buildings, and, in a few instances, even nuclear warheads.[9] There is an unimaginable amount of fraud and corruption at every level, and literally thousands of whistleblowers have tried to come forward every single year—one every six minutes. When they do take that incredibly brave action, over 90 percent of the claims are dismissed without even being investigated.

You would think, in this topsy-turvy world, if there were one organization we could trust with a trillion dollars a year of our taxpayer money, it would be the Department of Unauthorized Highly Secretive Mass Human Murder.

NOTES

1   See "The Pentagon Can't Account for 21 Trillion Dollars (That's Not a Typo)," in this volume.

2   Dave Lindorff, "The Pentagon's Massive Accounting Fraud Exposed," January 7, 2019, accessed September 25, 2019, https://www.thenation.

com/article/pentagon-audit-budget-fraud/; Laurence Kotlikoff, "Holding U.S. Treasurys? Beware: Uncle Sam Can't Account for $21 Trillion," *Forbes*, January 9, 2019, accessed September 25, 2019, https://www.forbes.com/sites/kotlikoff/2019/01/09/holding-u-s-treasuries-beware-uncle-sam-cant-account-for-21-trillion/#69be30aa7644; Alexandria Ocasio-Cortez (@AOC), "$21 TRILLION of Pentagon financial transactions 'could not be traced, documented, or explained,'" Twitter, December 2, 2018, accessed September 25, 2019, https://twitter.com/AOC/status/1069307293752279040.

3   Matt Taibbi, "The Pentagon's Bottomless Money Pit," *Rolling Stone*, March 17, 2019, accessed September 25, 2019, https://www.rollingstone.com/politics/politics-features/pentagon-budget-mystery-807276/.

4   Oriana Pawlyk, "Air Force No Longer Spending $10,000 on Toilet Seats, Officials Say," Military.com, July 11, 2018, accessed September 25, 2019, https://www.military.com/defensetech/2018/07/11/air-force-no-longer-spending-10000-toilet-seats-officials-say.html.

5   United States Government Accountability Office, "Whistleblower Protection: Analysis of DOD's Actions to Improve Case Timeliness and Safeguard Confidentiality," March 2019, accessed September 25, 2019, https://www.gao.gov/assets/700/697337.pdf.

6   David Pallister, "How the US Sent $12bn in Cash to Iraq. And Watched It Vanish," *Guardian*, February 7, 2007, accessed September 25, 2019, https://www.theguardian.com/world/2007/feb/08/usa.iraq1.

7   David DeGraw, "Pentagon: 95,613 Whistleblower Complaints, Trillions of Tax Dollars Unaccounted For," March 27, 2019, accessed September 25, 2019, https://degraw.media/pentagon-95613-whistleblower-complaints-trillions-of-tax-dollars-unaccounted-for/.

8   Scot J. Paltrow, "Special Report: The Pentagon's Doctored Ledgers Conceal Epic Waste," Reuters, November 18, 2013, accessed September 25, 2019, https://www.reuters.com/article/us-usa-pentagon-waste-specialreport-idusbre9aholq20131118.

9   Associated Press, "Air Force Official Fired after 6 Nukes Fly over U.S.," NBC News, accessed September 25, 2019, http://www.nbcnews.com/id/20427730/ns/us_news-military/t/air-force-official-fired-after-nukes-fly-over-us/#.XLSww6QpCbg.

EVERYONE HAS FALLEN FOR THE LIES ABOUT VENEZUELA

There are three things I know for sure in this fanciful, sometimes inglorious, experience we call life:

1. You will never have a safety pin when you need one, and you will have thousands when you don't need one.
2. Wild animals are breathtakingly majestic until they're crawling up your pant leg.
3. A US presidential administration will never admit that it invaded another country or backed a coup attempt in order to essentially steal the natural resources (oil) of said country.

This is why it was so very shocking last week when members of the Trump administration admitted they were backing a coup attempt in order to essentially steal the natural resources (oil) of another country.

That country is Venezuela. I'll get back to this in a moment.

Let's take a second to go over the *big three*. There are three things that seem to provoke the ornery United States into overthrowing or bringing down a foreign government, no matter how many innocent civilians may die in the process. (If enough die, the perpetrators often get nominated for a Nobel Peace Prize.) If your country has *one* of these things, the US might screw with you. If your country has two of these things, the US will *definitely* screw with you. If your country has *three* of these things, then look behind you, because the US is *currently* screwing you:

1.   Being socialist.
Pretty self-explanatory. If you don't have the same economic system as we do, we treat it like you have candy, and we're not allowed to have any, so we slip razor blades in yours and tell everyone your candy kills people.
2.   Dropping the US dollar.
Iraq dropped the dollar. We invaded.
Syria dropped the dollar. We invaded.
Iran dropped the dollar. We want to invade.
Libya dropped the dollar. We invaded.
Pakistan dropped the dollar in trade with China, and the following day the US added them to the list of countries violating religious freedom.[1] (I guess you could argue they did indeed violate *our* religion: the dollar.)
Basically, we do *not* take kindly to countries dropping the dollar.
In unrelated news, Venezuela dropped the dollar.[2]
3.   Having oil or other natural resources the US needs.
In case you were curious, Venezuela has the largest oil reserves in the known world.[3] (But we haven't checked northern Wyoming yet, because it's a long, cold drive with nary a 7-11.)

So these are the three *actual* reasons the US has created an attempted coup in Venezuela over the past several weeks. And right now, you are falling into one of two categories. Either you're saying to yourself, "Of course those are the reasons. Those are the only reasons the US *ever* tries to bring down governments." Or you still have some strange, deep-rooted faith in our Pepsi and pharmaceutical–owned media outlets, and therefore you're thinking, "That's not true. The US supports the opposition in Venezuela, because we want to help those poor starving people." But if that were accurate, we would be tripping over ourselves to help starving and sick people around the world. Instead we (oddly) only seek to help them when they have oil under their feet. And, in fact, data has proven this true. A study a few years ago from the Universities of Portsmouth, Warwick, and Essex found that foreign intervention in civil conflicts is 100 times more likely if the country has a great deal of oil, versus none.[4]

So who is feeding the average American the idea that our involvement in Venezuela is about helping people? Only *every* mainstream media channel in America—from MSNBC to Fox News to NPR to Bill fuckin' Maher. It's truly mind-numbing to watch so-called liberals march in lockstep with the likes of John Bolton, Elliott Abrams, Donald Trump, and every neocon not currently in a coma.

These outlets froth at the mouth while presenting segments explaining that the Venezuelan people are starving, but they also purposefully avoid mentioning that a lot of Venezuela's hardships are due to US sanctions.[5] This isn't to say Venezuela's president Nicolás Maduro has done an awesome job. But whether he has or not, saying we must sanction them to help them is like if somebody fell through a plate glass window and you said, "Let's help him! Let's start cutting the glass shards out of his skin with this rusty flathead screwdriver I found in an abandoned mine! Then we'll pour Mountain Dew and sewage water in the wounds to help them heal!"

But that's what our sanctions are designed to do. They're devised from day one to hurt poor and average people the most, to make them angry enough to rebel. Over a year ago, when Rex Tillerson was secretary of state, he publicly said we could tell our sanctions on North Korea were working great, because poor fishermen were washing up on the beaches starved to death.[6] (One is perplexed by how difficult it is at times to tell the difference between "helping other countries" and mass murder.)

Sanctions are not smart bombs. They destroy everybody, except the rich—who have enough money to weather the sanctions. Come to think of it, sanctions *are* kind of like smart bombs. We're told they're only going to hit the bad guys, but, in fact, "smart bombs" kill all kinds of innocent civilians, just like sanctions do.

Furthermore, the US "humanitarian aid" that we claim to be sending is not what it seems. Even NPR took a break from its traditional role as State Department stenographer-in-training to reveal that the "humanitarian aid" is actually meant to create regime change.[7] And McClatchy last week uncovered that the North Carolina–based private freight company 21 Air LLC has made 40 secretive flights to Venezuela from the US in the past month, and that the Venezuelan government claimed the flights were filled to the brim with assault weapons and ammunition destined for opposition forces.[8] (Apparently, we thought the Venezuelans were going to cook up a fresh pot of bullet stew to ease their hunger pains.) To make matters worse, two executives at the company have ties to an air cargo company that helped the CIA "rendition" supposed terrorists to black sites for "interrogation" (read: torture).[9]

The next piece of propaganda lovingly pedestalled by our mainstream media robot-heads is simply calling Juan Guaidó the "interim president," without mentioning that he was not elected to that position and only 30 out of 200 nations recognize him as such.[10] He just declared himself president. Last I checked, that's not really how governments work. But if it is—okay, I hereby declare myself governor of . . . let's say, Idaho. No one will really notice. I'm pretty sure the current governor is a hedgehog in a bow tie.

There are many other things CNN, MSNBC, Fox News, and all the rest don't want you to know about Juan Guaidó. For example, until he named himself president,[11] 81 percent of Venezuelans didn't even know who he was, according to a poll conducted by the Venezuela-based firm Hinterlaces.[12]

And he only won his own assembly seat with 26 percent of the vote. In order to win elections in any country, you often need more than 30 percent of the people to have heard of you. Pauly Shore has more name recognition among Venezuelans than Juan Guaidó.

On top of that, Guaidó went to George Washington University. As the Grayzone Project reported, "[In 2007, h]e moved to Washington, D.C., to enroll in the Governance and Political Management Program at George Washington under the tutelage of Venezuelan Luis Enrique Berrizbeitia, one of the top Latin American neoliberal economists. Berrizbeitia is a former executive director of the International Monetary Fund."[13]

Guaidó went to GW, trained under Mr. IMF, and then we declared him president of Venezuela. That's like studying at the WWE, training under Henry Kissinger, and then the US declares you the king of Japan.

But it doesn't stop there, according to the Grayzone Project: "Juan Guaidó is the product of a decade-long project overseen by Washington's elite regime change trainers. While posing as a champion of democracy, he has spent years at the forefront of a violent campaign of destabilization."[14] Furthermore, Guaidó has already said he wants to sell Venezuela's oil to foreign companies and let the IMF back in, which will drown the country in debt. So he's an American regime change pawn who was groomed by the IMF to take over Venezuela and give away their natural resources. What a catch. . . . But if this is what the Venezuelan people really want, then we should respect their wishes. The corporate media tells us this is what the people want, right?

Except that it's not.

"According to a study conducted in early January 2019 . . . 86 percent of Venezuelans would disagree with international military intervention," Grayzone's Ben Norton reported last month. "And 81 percent oppose the US sanctions that have gravely hurt the nation's economy."[15]

So, based on the Hinterlaces poll, most Venezuelans didn't know Guaidó until recently. Most Venezuelans still support Maduro, even if they believe corruption in the government has increased (whether you personally like Maduro or not doesn't matter), and most Venezuelans don't want military intervention or US sanctions. Yet CNN and NPR and Fox News and the BBC and every other corporate outlet will have you thinking everyone is starving to death, on their knees begging for America's democracy bombs to rain down like dollar bills at a strip club.

But maybe I'm wrong. Maybe those people really need our help, and US intervention will work out *great*—exactly like it did in Syria,
and Yemen
and Iraq
and Iran
and Afghanistan
and Chile
and Honduras
and Haiti
and Somalia
and Libya
and Guatemala
and Nicaragua
and Colombia
and Panama
and Fraggle Rock
and those tree forts where the *Ewoks* lived!

Now that we have a general understanding of the situation (and why Anderson Cooper is not keen to remind viewers what happened with Fraggle Rock in the early nineties), let's get back to the question of oil.

When I first started writing this, I didn't have *proof* the American government wanted Venezuela's oil; it was just a hunch. Kinda like if you put a balloon in a room with a porcupine, you have a hunch he'll pop the balloon. But I didn't have a quote from a top Trump administration official saying, "We'd like to take their oil."

Then national security adviser and Mustache of Doom John Bolton said, "Hold my beer." While on Fox News he stated clearly, "It will make a big difference to the United States economically if we could have American oil companies invest in and produce the oil capabilities in Venezuela."[16]

That's Beltway speak for "We want their oil."

For 20 years we've been trying to destroy Venezuela, and our government always gives the standard line: "We want to help the people. We care about their democracy. They have a lot of inflation, and that's why we need to drop our freedom bombs on their heads." They've trotted out that bullshit brigade under Bush, Obama, and now Trump. The officials never just say, "Yeah, there's like, tons of oil there, and we want it."

Yet here it is. The disguise of neoliberal world domination has come off. (Ironically, the fake mustache was yanked off to reveal a much larger mustache.)

Also, it's amazing how monotone and matter-of-fact Bolton is as he speaks. A US-backed coup often ends in terrible violence with tens of thousands of innocent people killed. It's truly heartbreaking, no matter which side you support. Sometimes it ends up with a brutal military junta taking control. Yet here is John Bolton discussing it the same way he would analyze whether to have chocolate fudge ice cream or apple pie for dessert. ("Hmmm, possible death of a hundred thousand people? That sounds good—I'll have that.")

This is all the more horrifying because these policies are decided by *unelected* maniacs like Elliot Abrams, Mike Pompeo, and John Bolton. Trump just named Abrams special envoy to Venezuela despite the fact the guy has a résumé that would make Josef Mengele blush. And what's even more jaw-dropping is watching the liberati like Rachel Maddow,[17] Bill Maher, and nearly every democrat in Congress get in line to support the talking points of right-wing warlords (the belligerati) like Bolton, Abrams, Pompeo, Trump, Hannity, and nearly every Republican in Congress. The mountains of propaganda put forward make it hard to breathe (the air is thinner up here).

Worse yet—even the *Wall Street Journal* stated the US push to oust Maduro is just the first shot in the oligarchy's plan to reshape Latin America.[18] It turns out sociopathy is addictive. Our American empire knows no bounds to its nation-building (after nation-destroying).

The Venezuelan people deserve self-determination, no matter how you feel about the current government. The absolute *last thing* they need is to be turned into a neocon/neoliberal parking lot in which America rips all their resources out from under them while calling it "freedom." Luckily, there are already many signs this US-created attempted coup is failing.[19]

NOTES

1   "U.S. Places Pakistan on Watch List for Religious Freedom Violations," Reuters, January 4, 2018, accessed September 25, 2019, https://www. reuters.com/article/us-usa-religion/u-s-places-pakistan-on-watch-list-for-religious-freedom-violations-idUSKBN1ET1OA.

2   Whitney Webb, "Venezuela Accused of Drug Trafficking after Dropping U.S. Petrodollar," MintPress News, September 18, 2017, accessed September 25, 2019, https://www.mintpressnews.com/venezuela-drops-petrodollar-us-sanctions-drug-trafficking/232056/.

3   Daniel J. Graeber, "Venezuela Is the Clear Global Leader in Oil Reserves," UPI, July 31, 2018, accessed September 25, 2019, https://www.upi.com/Venezuela-is-the-clear-global-leader-in-oil-reserves/9251533031601/.

4   Tom Bawden, "Intervention in Civil Wars 'Far More Likely in Oil-Rich Nations,'" *Independent*, January 28, 2015, accessed September 25, 2019, https://www.independent.co.uk/news/world/middle-east/intervention-in-civil-wars-far-more-likely-in-oil-rich-nations-10006648.html.

5   Alex Campbell, "The Truth about US Sanctions on Venezuela, and Why the Media Gets It Wrong," MintPress News, February 5, 2019, accessed September 25, 2019, https://www.mintpressnews.com/the-truth-about-us-sanctions-on-venezuela-and-whys-the-media-gets-it-wrong/254625/.

6   Redacted Tonight, "Sec. of State Says U.S. Should Celebrate Starving People," YouTube, January 31, 2018, accessed September 25, 2019, https://www.youtube.com/watch?v=AlQNcjZu2RU.

7   John Otis, "U.S. Masses Aid along Venezuelan Border as Some Humanitarian Groups Warn of Risks," February 16, 2019, accessed September 25, 2019, https://www.npr.org/2019/02/16/695154567/u-s-masses-aid-along-venezuelan-border-as-some-humanitarian-groups-warn-of-risks.

8   Tim Johnson, "Venezuela Says Plane from Miami Delivered Weapons for Use by Enemies of Maduro," McClatchy, February 7, 2019, accessed September 25, 2019, https://www.mcclatchydc.com/news/nation-world/world/latin-america/article225949200.html.

9   Martin Vassolo, Tim Johnson, and David Ovalle, "Air Charter Firm, Client Both Deny Role in Alleged Shipment of Arms to Venezuela," McClatchy, February 8, 2019, accessed September 25, 2019, https://www.mcclatchydc.com/news/nation-world/national/national-security/article226011940.html.

10   Margaret Flowers and Kevin Zeese, "The Rise of a Fake President in Venezeula," PopularResistance.org, February 4, 2019, accessed September 25, 2019, https://popularresistance.org/the-rise-of-a-fake-president-in-venezuela/.

11   Alison Bodine, "Imperialist Aggression & What We Can Learn from the Attempted Coup against Venezuela," PopularResistance.org, February 14, 2019, accessed September 25, 2019, https://popularresistance.org/imperialist-aggression-what-we-can-learn-from-the-attempted-coup-against-venezuela/.

12   "¡Oposición sin liderazgo! 81% de los venezolanos no sabe quién es Juan Guaidó (+ Encuesta)," Con el Mazo Dando, January 20, 2019, accessed September 25, 2019, https://www.conelmazodando.com.ve/oposicion-sin-liderazgo-81-de-los-venezolanos-no-sabe-quien-es-juan-guaido-encuesta.

13   Dan Cohen and Max Blumenthal, "The Making of Juan Guaidó: How the US Regime Change Laboratory Created Venezuela's Coup Leader," Grayzone, January 29, 2019, accessed September 25, 2019, https://grayzoneproject.com/2019/01/29/the-making-of-juan-guaido-how-the-us-regime-change-laboratory-created-venezuelas-coup-leader/.

14   Ibid.

15   Ben Norton, "86% of Venezuelans Oppose Military Intervention, 81% against US Sanctions, Local Polling Shows," Grayzone, January 29, 2019, accessed September 25, 2019, https://grayzoneproject.com/2019/01/29/venezuelans-oppose-intervention-us-sanctions-poll/.

16   Ben Norton, "US Coup in Venezuela Motivated by Oil and Corporate Interests—Militarist John Bolton Spills the Beans," Grayzone, January 29, 2019, accessed September 25, 2019, https://grayzoneproject. com/2019/01/29/us-coup-venezuela-oil-corporate-john-bolton/.

17   Adam Johnson, "MSNBC's 'Resistance' to Trump's Venezuela Coup Ranges from Silence to Support," FAIR, February 13, 2019, accessed September 25, 2019, https://fair.org/home/action-alert-msnbcs-resistance-to-trumps-venezuela-coup-ranges-from-silence-to-support/.

18   Jessica Donati, Vivian Salama, and Ian Talley, "U.S. Push to Oust Venezuela's Maduro Marks First Shot in Plan to Reshape Latin America," Wall St. Journal, January 30, 2019, accessed September 25, 2019, https://www.wsj.com/articles/u-s-push-to-oust-venezuelas-maduro-marks-first-shot-in-plan-to-reshape-latin-america-11548888252.

19   Staff, Moonofalabama.org, "Venezuela—Media Find Trump's Coup Plan Does Not Work," PopularResistance.org, February 16, 2019, accessed September 25, 2019, https://popularresistance.org/venezuela-media-find-trumps-coup-plan-does-not-work/.

ARTIFICIAL INTELLIGENCE MAY DESTROY HUMANITY BY ACCIDENT (BUT IT WON'T APOLOGIZE)

The US military has quietly said it wants 70 unmanned self-driving supply trucks by 2020.[1] And seeing as 21 trillion dollars have gone unaccounted for at the Pentagon over the past 20 years, when the Pentagon wants something, it tends to get that something.[2]

Of course, supply trucks in and of themselves don't sound so bad. Even if the self-driving trucks run over some poor unsuspecting saps, that will still be the *least* destruction our military has *ever* manifested. But because I've read a thing or two about our military, I'll assume that by "supply trucks," they mean "ruthless killing machines." In fact, it's now clear the entire "Department of Defense" is just a rebranding of "Department of Ruthless Killing Machines."

And even if they *do* mean simple supply trucks, once those unmanned trucks are commuting themselves around the Middle East like a cross between *Driving Miss Daisy* and *Platoon*, how long do you think it will be until some a-hole general blurts, "Why don't we put a missile or two on those things?"

The answer is 17 minutes. (Fifteen minutes if Trump is still president.)

Plus, these trucks are not the military's only venture into artificial intelligence. The Navy wants 13.5 million dollars to go toward rapid advances in AI.[3] The Air Force is looking for 87 million dollars to experiment with it. The Army has requested 6.5 million dollars more for it. And the Marine Corps says it needs 7.1 million dollars. (These are just the *publicly stated* numbers. Much like a vampire, our military does 95 percent of its best work in the dark.)

So this brings up a pressing question that we will see again and again in the coming years: How much do we need to fear artificial intelligence—or is it simply a great technological advancement?

Let me answer that question with a bit of a tangent. Human beings are notoriously unreliable. But there are two things you can *always* rely on humans for:

1. Humans will advance technology in every way possible.
2. Other humans will strap explosives to that technology.

Think about it: The automobile eventually became the tank. The airplane became the bomber. The printing press became the semi-automatic assault printing press. And so on.

But maybe I'm being paranoid. Maybe artificial intelligence is here to help us. One of the top AI geniuses at Google says the world is currently screwed (climate change, pollution, Auto-Tune). To save it, he says:

> either we need an exponential improvement in human behavior—less selfishness, less short-termism, more collaboration, more generosity—or we need an exponential improvement in technology. . . . I don't think we're going to be getting an exponential improvement in human behavior. . . . That's why we need a quantum leap in technology like AI.[4]

Basically, he's saying we're horrible, shitty people who are not going to change, but the bots will arrive soon to show us the way!

And there is some truth to this. AI will one day be able to tap into basically the entire internet simultaneously and learn everything that has ever been learned far quicker than troglodytes like us. So it will be incredibly, unimaginably smart and will always be three moves ahead of us. On top of that, it won't have the things that get in the way of our mental advancement as a species, such as:

- hunger
- fear
- insecurity
- superstition
- religion
- the drive to stick one's penis in anything that moves.

Artificial intelligence doesn't have to deal with any of that.

So maybe AI will indeed save us from ourselves. . . . Orrrr, maybe with its infinite knowledge it will decide the planet would be better off without the ape-like creatures who keep trying to tell it what to do. Tesla CEO Elon Musk had an exciting and upbeat response when he was recently asked about how fast artificial intelligence is advancing. "I tried to convince people to slow down. Slow down AI, to regulate AI. This was futile. I tried for years."[5] (If you happen to have a cyanide tablet nearby, now would be the time to chomp down on that.)

Musk believes artificial intelligence is a far greater threat to humanity than nuclear weapons. Keep in mind, in order for AI to do great harm to our dopey species, it doesn't necessarily have to be out to get us. It could simply come up with "solutions" that humans aren't really prepared for. Here's an example from the *Atlantic* of an AI mistake:

> One algorithm was supposed to figure out how to land a virtual airplane with minimal force. But the AI soon discovered that if it crashed the plane, the program would register a force so large that it would overwhelm its memory and count it as a perfect score. So the AI crashed the plane, over and over again, killing all the virtual people on board.[6]

That particular bot got a perfect score on landing a plane by killing all the imaginary humans. It kind of reminds me of the time I stopped my younger brother from beating me in *The Legend of Zelda* video game by throwing our television in a creek.

So now, dear reader, you may be thinking, "That's terrifying—the AI was given an objective and basically just did *anything* to get there." However, is that so different from humans? In our society, we are given the objective of "accumulate wealth and power," and now we have people like weapons contractors and big oil magnates achieving the objective by promoting and fostering war and death around the world. It's almost like they don't care how they achieve the objective.

I'm not saying I know whether AI will save us all or kill us all, but I am saying these are the types of questions that need to be asked, *and soon*, because we won't be the smartest beings on this planet much longer. (As it is, we're barely holding on to the top spot. A solid 50 percent of us are just glorified butlers to our dogs and cats. One can't really claim to rule the world when one is carrying the poop of another species.)

NOTES

1   Sydney J. Freedberg Jr., "Army Wants 70 Self-Driving Supply Trucks by 2020," Breaking Defense, August 20, 2018, accessed September 25, 2019, https://breakingdefense.com/2018/08/army-wants-70-self-driving-supply-trucks-by-2020/.

2   Laurence Kotlikoff, "Is Our Government Intentionally Hiding $21 Trillion in Spending?" *Forbes*, July 21, 2018, accessed September 24, 2019, https://www.forbes.com/sites/kotlikoff/2018/07/21/is-our-government-intentionally-hiding-21-trillion-in-spending/#2b9a00ca4a73.

3   Brandon Knapp, "Here's Where the Pentagon Wants to Invest in Artificial Intelligence in 2019," C4ISRNET, February 16, 2018, accessed September 25, 2019, https://www.c4isrnet.com/intel-geoint/2018/02/16/heres-where-the-pentagon-wants-to-invest-in-artificial-intelligence-in-2019/.

4   Nick Heath, "Google DeepMind Founder Demis Hassabis: Three Truths about AI," TechRepublic, September 24, 2018, accessed September 25, 2019, https://www.techrepublic.com/article/google-deepmind-founder-demis-hassabis-three-truths-about-ai/.

5   Redacted Tonight, "~214~ Military AI Takeover, Dollar Crashing, Facial Scans," YouTube, October 6, 2018, accessed September 25, 2019, https://youtu.be/XnlAkTR6GcA?t=275.

6   Derek Thompson, "The Spooky Genius of Artificial Intelligence," *The Atlantic*, September 28, 2018, accessed September 25, 2019, https://www.theatlantic.com/ideas/archive/2018/09/can-artificial-intelligence-be-smarter-than-a-human-being/571498/.

TRUMP'S MILITARY DROPS A BOMB EVERY 12 MINUTES, AND NO ONE IS TALKING ABOUT IT

We live in a state of perpetual war, and we never feel it. While you get your gelato at the hip place where they put those cute little mint leaves on the side, someone is being bombed in your name. While you argue with the 17-year-old at the movie theater who gave you a small popcorn when you paid for a large, someone is being obliterated in your name. While we sleep and eat and make love and shield our eyes on a sunny day, someone's home, family, life, and body are being blown into a thousand pieces—in our names.

Once every 12 minutes.

The United States military drops an explosive with a strength you can hardly comprehend once every 12 minutes. And that's odd, because we're technically at war with—let me think—zero countries. So that should mean zero bombs are being dropped, right?

Hell no! You've made the common mistake of confusing our world with some sort of rational, cogent world in which our military-industrial complex is under control, the music industry is based on merit and talent, Legos have gently rounded edges (so when you step on them barefoot, it doesn't feel like an armor-piercing bullet just shot straight up your sphincter), and humans are dealing with climate change like adults rather than burying our heads in the sand, while trying to convince ourselves that the sand around our heads isn't getting *really hot*.

You're thinking of a rational world. We do not live there.

Instead, we live in a world where the Pentagon is completely and utterly out of control. President George W. Bush's military dropped 70 thousand bombs on five countries.[1] But of that outrageous number, only 57 of those bombs really upset the international community.

Because there were 57 strikes in Pakistan, Somalia, and Yemen—countries the US was neither at war with nor had ongoing conflicts with. And the world was kind of horrified. There was a lot of talk that went something like, "Wait a second. We're bombing in countries outside of war zones? Is it possible that's a slippery slope ending in us just bombing all the goddamn time? (Awkward pause.) . . . Nah. Whichever president follows Bush will be a normal adult person (with a functional brain stem of some sort) and will, therefore, stop this madness."

We were so cute and naive back then, like a kitten when it's first waking up in the morning.

The Bureau of Investigative Journalism reported that under President Barack Obama there were "563 strikes, largely by drones, that targeted Pakistan, Somalia and Yemen."[2]

It's not just the fact that bombing outside of a war zone is a horrific violation of international law and global norms. It's also the morally reprehensible targeting of people for "pre-crime," which is what we're doing and what the Tom Cruise movie *Minority Report* warned us about. (Humans are very bad at taking the advice of sci-fi dystopias. If we'd listened to 1984, we wouldn't have allowed the existence of the National Security Agency. If we'd listened to *The Terminator*, we wouldn't have allowed the existence of drone warfare. And if we'd listened to *The Matrix*, we wouldn't have allowed the vast majority of humans to get lost in a virtual reality of spectacle and vapid nonsense while the oceans die in a swamp of plastic waste.[3] . . . But you know, who's counting?)

There was basically a media blackout while Obama was president. You could count on one hand the number of mainstream media reports on the Pentagon's daily bombing campaign under Obama. And even when the media did mention it, the underlying sentiment was, "Yeah, but look at how suave Obama is while he's okaying endless destruction. He's like the Steve McQueen of aerial death."

And let's take a moment to wipe away the idea that our "advanced weaponry" hits only the bad guys. As David DeGraw put it, "According to the C.I.A.'s own documents, the people on the 'kill list,' who were targeted for 'death-by-drone,' accounted for only 2% of the deaths caused by the drone strikes."[4]

Two percent. Really, Pentagon? You got a two on the test? You get five points just for spelling your name right.

But those 70 thousand bombs dropped by Bush—it was child's play. DeGraw again: "[Obama] dropped 100,000 bombs in seven countries. He out-bombed Bush by 30,000 bombs and 2 countries."[5]

You have to admit that's impressively horrific. That puts Obama in a very elite group of Nobel Peace Prize winners who have killed that many innocent civilians. The reunions are mainly just him and Henry Kissinger wearing little hand-drawn name tags and munching on deviled eggs.

However, we now know that Donald Trump's administration puts all previous presidential administrations to shame. The Pentagon's numbers show that during George W. Bush's eight years he averaged 24 bombs dropped per day, which is 8,750 per year. Over the course of Obama's time in office, his military dropped 34 bombs per day, 12,500 per year. And in Trump's first year in office, he averaged 121 bombs dropped per day, for an annual total of 44,096.

Trump's military dropped 44 thousand bombs in his first year in office.

He has basically taken the gloves off the Pentagon, taken the leash off an already rabid dog. So the end result is a military that's behaving like Lil Wayne crossed with Conor McGregor. You look away for one minute, look back, and are like, "What the fuck did you just do? I was gone for, like, a second!"

Under Trump, five bombs are dropped per hour—every hour of every day. That averages out to a bomb every 12 minutes.

And which is more outrageous—the crazy amount of death and destruction we are creating around the world, or the fact that your mainstream corporate media basically NEVER investigates it? They talk about Trump's flaws. They say he's a racist, bulbous-headed, self-centered idiot (which is totally accurate)—but they don't criticize the perpetual Amityville massacre our military perpetrates by dropping a bomb every 12 minutes, most of them killing 98 percent nontargets.

When you have a Department of War with a completely unaccountable budget—as we saw with the 21 trillion dollars—and you have a president with no interest in overseeing how much death the Department of War is responsible for, then you end up dropping so many bombs that the Pentagon has reported we are running out of bombs.[6]

Oh, dear god. If we run out of our bombs, then how will we stop all those innocent civilians from . . . farming? Think of all the goats that will be allowed to go about their days.

And, as with the 21 trillion dollars, the theme seems to be "unaccountable."

Journalist Whitney Webb wrote in February:

> Shockingly, more than 80 percent of those killed have never even been identified and the C.I.A.'s own documents have shown that they are not even aware of who they are killing—avoiding the issue of reporting civilian deaths simply by naming all those in the strike zone as enemy combatants.[7]

That's right. We kill only enemy combatants. How do we know they're enemy combatants? Because they were in our strike zone. How did we know it was a strike zone? Because there were enemy combatants there. How did we find out they were enemy combatants? Because they were in the strike zone. . . . Want me to keep going, or do you get the point? I have all day.

This is not about Trump, even though he's a maniac. It's not about Obama, even though he's a war criminal. It's not about Bush, even though he has the intelligence of boiled cabbage. (I haven't told a Bush joke in about eight years. Felt kind of good. Maybe I'll get back into that.)

This is about a runaway military-industrial complex that our ruling elite are more than happy to let loose. Almost no one in Congress or the presidency tries to restrain our 121 bombs a day. Almost no one in a mainstream outlet tries to get people to care about this.

Recently, the hashtag #21Trillion for the unaccounted Pentagon money has gained some traction. Let's get another one started: #121BombsADay.

One every 12 minutes.

Do you know where they're hitting? Who they're murdering? Why? One hundred and twenty-one bombs a day rip apart the lives of families a world away—in your name and my name and the name of the kid doling out the wrong size popcorn at the movie theater.

We are a rogue nation with a rogue military and a completely unaccountable ruling elite. The government and military you and I support by being a part of this society are murdering people every 12 minutes, and, in response, there's nothing but a ghostly silence. It is beneath us as a people and a species to give this topic nothing but silence. It is a crime against humanity.

NOTES

1   Nicolas J.S. Davies, "Obama's Bombing Legacy," Consortium News, January 18, 2017, accessed September 25, 2019, https:// consortiumnews.com/2017/01/18/obamas-bombing-legacy/.

2   Jessica Purkiss and Jack Serle, "Obama's Covert Drone War in Numbers: Ten Times More Strikes than Bush," Bureau of Investigative Journalism, January 17, 2017, accessed September 25, 2019, https://www.thebureauinvestigates.com/stories/2017-01-17/obamas-covert-drone-war-in-numbers-ten-times-more-strikes-than-bush.

3   Graeme Wearden, "More Plastic than Fish in the Sea by 2050, Says Ellen MacArthur," *Guardian*, January 19, 2016, accessed September 25, 2019, https://www.theguardian.com/business/2016/jan/19/more-plastic-than-fish-in-the-sea-by-2050-warns-ellen-macarthur.

4   David DeGraw, *Global War Profiteers vs. the People of the United States* (DeGraw Media, 2018), 60, accessed September 25, 2019, https://degraw.media/wp-content/uploads/2019/02/Global-War-Profiteers-Vs-The-People-of-the-United-States.pdf.

5   DeGraw, *Global War Profiteers vs. the People of the United States*.

6   Aaron Mehta, "The US Is Running Out of Bombs—and It May Soon Struggle to Make More," Defense News, May 22, 2018, accessed September 25, 2019, https://www.defensenews.com/pentagon/2018/05/22/the-us-is-running-out-of-bombs-and-it-may-soon-struggle-to-make-more/.

7   Whitney Webb, "Trump's Drone Kill Rate 80 Times Greater than under Bush," MintPress News, February 2, 2018, accessed September 25, 2019, https://www.mintpressnews.com/trumps-drone-kill-rate-80-times-greater-than-under-bush/237075/.

THE MEDIA NEVER MENTION THE NUMBER ONE CAUSE OF CLIMATE CHANGE

There are many issues the corporate media will debate in its standard, convoluted, manipulative manner. In fact, most issues will at some point get an hour of glowing fame on the mind control box. Yet some topics are forbidden, banned from discussion on the mainstream news channels.

One of those issues just happens to be the number one cause of manmade climate change and a top cause of illness, sickness, torture, and environmental destruction in the United States and around the world. So it's concerning that corporate media avoid it as if it's a highly unstable radioactive material being handed to them by Bill Cosby.

That topic is animal agriculture—the raising of the animals most of us eat.

Unlike the media, I do want to get into this topic—partially because it's hugely important and partially because I enjoy doing things that piss off corporate propaganda networks. But first, I think it will behoove us to go through a brief history of the world:

- Animal evolved into man.
- Man realized he could eat animal.
- Man caught and cooked animal.
- Man began housing animal before eating it, so that

he could have dinner waiting around whenever he wanted it—"fast food" before cars existed.

- Man realized he liked the way animal tasted when lightly fried and sprinkled on top of salads, pasta, soups, chocolate, *anything*.
- To keep up with demand, man began housing animal in smaller and smaller cages until man had millions of animals on top of each other living their entire lives in the most disgusting, immoral, vomit inducing manner.
- Man called anyone who pointed out how awful this is a "pussy."
- This was insulting to all animals and all women and, therefore, only made *man* look like a damn idiot.
- At that point we realized evolution doesn't always go in a direct line. Sometimes, it forks off into "what the fuck" land.

But I *don't* want to make this column about how animal agriculture is the largest cause of greenhouse gas emissions (or number two, depending on who you ask).[1]

Or how it requires the use of more than 190 billion gallons of water daily.[2] Yes, that's per day.

Or how it takes up 55 percent of our fresh water, compared with the only 5 percent used in households.[3]

Or the fact that according to the *Georgetown Environmental Law Review*, "Ocean dead zones. Fisheries depletion. Species extinction. Deforestation. World hunger. Food safety. Heart disease. Obesity. Diabetes. There is one issue at the heart of all these problems . . . our demand for and reliance on animal products."[4]

Or how it creates lagoons filled with millions of tons of feces that in North Carolina the Legislature made sure could legally be sprayed into the air, coating nearby townspeople.[5]

I don't want to talk about any of that, even though "Shit Lagoon" was also Mitch McConnell's nickname in high school. Nope, don't want to talk about it this time. Instead, let's discuss how awful our factory farming is for the animals, because, yes, cows are people too.

But let's start with hens—where most of our eggs come from. As the Intercept reported, "Nearly 280 million laying hens in the United States are confined in barren wire battery cages so restrictive the birds can't even spread their wings."[6]

These hens have less room than the surface of an iPad to live their entire lives (which I guess makes them similar to humans, since we now live our entire existence on the surface of an iPad). Point is, next time you're looking for a good horror movie—something to really make you piss your pants—grab some popcorn, put your arm around your lover and watch undercover videos of factory farming. (Either that or watch Chuck Schumer give a speech and try to force fake compassion from his dead eyes.)

After videos of these mass animal torture farms started making the rounds on YouTube, Americans had an odd reaction—they stopped wanting to eat the gross brown flesh coming out of the little piggy Guantanamo Bays. Then the torture farm corporations did exactly what you think they would do—which is exactly the most horrible thing they could do.

They passed laws making filming factory farms a crime (because when something is morally reprehensible, beating up or arresting the camera guy usually solves the problem— kind of like how murder is totally rad if you just don't take a selfie next to the body).[7] But it didn't work, because videos still leaked out. So now the corporate goons moved on to the next step—in some states, poultry industry lobbyists are trying to force through legislation that would mandate that stores carry their products.[8]

A couple months ago, Iowa's House of Representatives overwhelmingly passed a bill that says that "if a grocery store carries an inventory of specialty eggs for retail sale, it must also carry an inventory of conventional eggs (shell eggs that are not considered specialty eggs)."[9]

This begs the question, "What are specialty eggs? Do they have little knitted sweaters on or what?" Well, "specialty eggs" means eggs that were *not* obtained through horrific end-of-days medieval torture. So "specialty eggs" basically means free-range—shouldn't that be called *normal* eggs? Eggs that come from a hen just standing out in a field—shouldn't that be called a "conventional egg"? And then the other eggs should be called "holy shit what a sick species we are eggs"?

Anyway, this law forces stores to sell eggs they and their customers find morally repulsive. That would be like a store owner saying, "Yeah, I'm not selling the supersonic, earthquake-level, vibrating triple dong at my adult toy store because people were getting injured and breaking hips and stuff." And then the state coming in and going, "Sorry, we had a talk with the earthquake triple dong lobbyists, and they're very powerful. So we're going to make it illegal for you *not* to sell it in your store."

I'm no free-market evangelist, but this sounds like the opposite of a free market.

By the way, our mainstream media won't mention the gruesome way our meat and eggs are produced, but they'll show ads endlessly telling you how awesome meat is. "Try our fluffy egg-wich with a bacon milkshake!" Those ads don't mention that the World Health Organization says that processed meats cause cancer, high blood pressure, and heart disease.[10]

Eating torture-farmed meat doesn't even make sense to most people who do it. If you show people a bird trapped in an oil spill, most of us want to save it. We want to help it. We want to break out the Dawn soap and shine that mallard's forehead until you can see your damn reflection in it.

But, for some reason, if that were a tanker full of barbecue sauce that tipped over, we'd be fine with it. We'd be downright excited. It would be declared a delicious disaster.

There's no logic in voraciously continuing a behavior that will kill us in both the short and long term *and* doesn't add up with our views toward animals. We have laws against animal abuse—as long as it's one of the animals we've been socially engineered to protect. If you see someone smack a Labrador Retriever in public, you'll dive in front of it like you're the Secret Service taking a bullet for the president. But if you replace that dog with a pig or a lamb, then we all think, "Grill 'em up! What kind of sauce you got for that?"

If it wasn't for aggressive cultural programming, our meat-eating habits would seem utterly crazy, like Groundhog Day or circumcision. You've got to have that weird stuff pounded into your head early, or you would never buy it. The truth is that we will look back on corporate torture farming as nearly as horrific as slavery or child brides or the sitcom ALF. We'll be like, "What the actual fuck were we thinking?"

Granted, there was a time when we needed to eat the meat that was around, or we would die. During horrible blizzards in the 1600s, many a trusted horse learned the hard way that we would bite into anything when push came to shove. But modern times are different. We *have* food. We have year-round ripe mangos that don't even make natural sense. There's no need to keep 280 million hens and 68 million pigs in a fucking *Saw* movie.[11]

Most people knew deep down that slavery was wrong, but they were fed dozens of different reasons to keep it going. They were told all kinds of crap science, crap history, and distorted Bible verses. Now imagine if—on top of that—in the 1800s, there had been television commercials constantly inundating the public with how great slavery is. How it's normal and wonderful and delicious and you can sprinkle slavery on top of your chocolate. Would it have lasted another 30 or 50 years? Maybe. (Oh crap, chocolate is still made with slave labor.[12] That kind of hurts my point, but I still think you get it.)

Our illogical, immoral meat consumption will kill our planet, kill our future, and possibly kill your family. And some might say it's probably not so good for your being, your energy, or your life force to fill your body with the tortured corpses of nonhuman sentient beings. Do you really want your body to be a Voltron made up of abused cows and beaten pigs? (I don't buy that hippie stuff, but if it works for you, go with it.)

Look, you don't have to quit meat. I know it's hard. Just decrease the amount you eat a little each month. Or do what I do—I eat only meat that's hard to get. Endangered species. That's it. Just platypus, pygmy hippos, and baby echidna puggles.

And I eat only free-range baby echidna puggles. I'm not a supervillain.

NOTES

1   "The Facts," Cowspiracy, accessed September 25, 2019, http://www. cowspiracy.com/facts/.

2   Liv Hanewald, "Animal Agriculture Is the Leading Cause of Climate Change," Odyssey, December 12, 2017, accessed September 25, 2019, https://www.theodysseyonline.com/animal-agriculture-the-leading-cause-of-climate-change.

3   "The Facts."

4   Christopher Hyner, "A Leading Cause of Everything: One Industry That Is Destroying Our Planet and Our Ability to Thrive on It," *Harvard Environmental Law Review*, October 26, 2015, accessed September 25, 2019, https://harvardelr.com/2015/10/26/elrs-a-leading-cause-of-everything-one-industry-that-is-destroying-our-planet-and-our-ability-to-thrive-on-it/ .

5   Erica Hellerstein and Ken Fine, "A Million Tons of Feces and an Unbearable Stench: Life Near Industrial Pig Farms," *Guardian*, September 20, 2017, accessed September 25, 2019, https://www. theguardian.com/us-news/2017/sep/20/north-carolina-hog-industry-pig-farms.

6   Glenn Greenwald and Leighton Akio Woodhouse, "Consumers Are Revolting against Animal Cruelty—So the Poultry Industry Is Lobbying for Laws to Force Stores to Sell Their Eggs," Intercept, March 2, 2018, accessed September 25, 2019, https://theintercept. com/2018/03/02/consumers-are-revolting-against-animal-cruelty-so-the-poultry-industry-is-lobbying-for-laws-to-force-stores-to-sell-their-eggs/.

7   Richard A. Oppel, "Taping of Farm Cruelty Is Becoming the Crime," *New York Times*, April 6, 2013, accessed September 25, 2019, http://www.nytimes.com/2013/04/07/us/taping-of-farm-cruelty-is-becoming-the-crime.html.

8   Greenwald and Woodhouse, "Consumers Are Revolting against Animal Cruelty."

9   Iowa House Bill 2408, LegiScan, March 21, 2018, accessed September 25, 2019, https://legiscan.com/IA/text/HF2408/id/1736129.

10 Stacy Simon, "World Health Organization Says Processed Meat Causes Cancer," American Cancer Society, October 26, 2015, accessed September 25, 2019, https://www.cancer.org/latest-news/world-health-organization-says-processed-meat-causes-cancer.html.

11 Greenwald and Woodhouse, "Consumers Are Revolting against Animal Cruelty."

12 "Child Labor in the Chocolate Industry," Food Empowerment Project, accessed September 25, 2019, http://www.foodispower.org/slavery-chocolate/.

OUR PLANET'S WONDERS NEVER CEASE

Science found a fish without a face.

(And, I swear to god, if anybody makes a Nicolas Cage/ John Travolta joke, I will punch them . . . not in the face.)

I say "science found a fish without a face," because if you or I or any Homo sapiens found a fish without a face, we would just post it on Instagram with the caption "WTF!!" followed by a second photo of said person enjoying a lovely blackened faceless fish taco. (Then again, I guess all fish tacos are faceless fish tacos. . . . Or, rather, one hopes.)

So science found a fish without a face off the coast of Australia. And it turns out they had found it once before a hundred years ago (at which time we were a little less jaded and it was just added to the list titled "Holy fucking Christ, what the fuck is out there?"). This fish has no discernible eyes or nose, and its mouth is farther down underneath its body. So, all told, it basically looks like a very large back half of a fish decided to keep making a go of it long after its head departed for warmer waters.

I have to admit that my first thought when confronted with a faceless fish is, "Maybe we can genetically combine it with Donald Trump, thereby creating a Captain Asshole without a face. This would hopefully make the number of idiotic country-embarrassing things he says decrease in number." (I say his comments embarrass the country, but, really, they embarrass the world and perhaps the species and perhaps carbon-based lifeforms and perhaps physical matter. Let's be honest.)

My second thought was, "Wow, what a lucky fish. It will never have to hear Justin Bieber, Brian Stelter, or Nancy Pelosi. And that's the best gig a conscious lifeform could get, with the possible exception of faceless fish taster." (I assume they taste amazing because they've never had Justin Bieber tunes tainting their flesh.)

But my third thought is the one that matters. It is: Isn't this planet breathtaking? Despite all we've done to it, despite all our bullshit and pollution, despite all our wars and aggression, despite all our *crap* . . . isn't spaceship Earth awe-inspiring? It still has the ability to amaze and bewilder. There are still species we haven't found and animals designed in such a manner that they shock us. While we bicker over religion and race and money (a figment of our imagination that some are willing to kill for)—while we fight over all that, this poetic planet is still doing what it does best: being majestic. And it's our job to create a sustainable future in which we can keep appreciating that majesty, in which we can keep having our minds blown by fish without faces.

THE MAINSTREAM MEDIA IS LYING ABOUT THE CALIFORNIA FIRES

I don't like accurately predicting the future. But it happens to me sometimes. And it's never a good thing.

Not once have I predicted that I would stumble upon a great sum of money or that a friendly squirrel would mysteriously leave a fresh, delicious scone on my windowsill. No, the things I've said that have come true years later have always been utterly awful. And the latest one has to do with California.

This week, Donald Trump has continued to blame the horrific fires in California on forest mismanagement—basically saying that if the parks service had just raked up a few more dry leaves, then countless people, homes, and buildings would not have been incinerated.[1] I unintentionally predicted this kind of idiocy. I said something similar on a 2011 stand-up comedy album titled *Chaos for the Weary*.

To paraphrase, I said, "You notice no matter how close they say the major effects of global warming are, it doesn't change how we all behave? Soon they'll be saying, 'People in California are *on fire*!' and everyone will be like, 'They probably live in a very fiery area. They're probably storing dry stuff in their homes—like old magazines and elderly people.'"

And sure enough, here we are. People in California are aflame, and the president is saying it's because they stored too many dry pine needles around their homes. Trump is able to do this because most of the mainstream media are allowing him to fill a void—a void that represents the answer to these questions: "Why is this happening? Why is our nation turning into one of the lower circles of hell?"

Don't get me wrong—the corporate media *have* extensively covered the fact that California is burning. They have. They just can't bring themselves to say the words "climate change" very often. No. It gets caught in their throat like a dry falafel puck. They look like they want to say it but just can't—like a dog that wants to tell you it has a thorn in its paw. But it's just impossible.

Take, for example, *NBC Nightly News*. You can't get a finer news program anywhere (in the building where they tape). I watched a full six-minute segment last week covering multiple California fires, the destruction, the loss of life; they even had reporters on the ground. Yet throughout the entire report, they never uttered the words "climate change," "global warming," or even simply, "We are fucked." Instead, they made it sound like fires are a tragic yet common occurrence, and the cities will rebuild.

Never speaking the words "climate change," while whole towns literally go up in flames, is like covering the drowning death of someone and never mentioning he was being waterboarded at the time. The *real* cause of these fires is at least half the story, if not more.

NBC host Kate Snow did say these fires are "ones for the history books," but I guess those books are going to get shorter and shorter because a "once every 1,000 years" fire is quickly becoming a "once every five years" fire. Saying these fires are "ones for the history books" implies that 20 years from now, the children in California will be reading about the "great fires" of 2018.

But they won't.

They won't be in the history books—because in 20 years the history books will be *on fire*. And the great fires of 2018 will look like nothing but a warm day with a piña colada. Here's an example of what I mean: a headline from the Huffington Post read, "California's Wildfires This Year Have Been Breaking Records: The State Has Experienced Some of the Biggest and Deadliest Fires in Its History This Year."[2]

Sounds pretty accurate, doesn't it? The only problem is that article is from December 2017. Did they go down in the history books? How often does everyone huddle under the blankets and take turns telling scary tales about the 2017 fires?

Acting like each year's fires are a fluke that will never happen again—that, in and of itself, is denying climate change. It is lying to the American people in order to cover up the fact that we are promoting a system based on big oil, big factory farming, and big environmental destruction. A new Media Matters report found the mainstream media only say "climate change" in reports about these recent fires 4 percent of the time.[3]

Now, some of you may be thinking, "You can't prove these fires were caused by climate change." And you're right. I can't. But the Union of Concerned Scientists can.

They said, "The effects of global warming on temperature, precipitation levels, and soil moisture are turning many of our forests into kindling during wildfire season." The scientists also pointed out that wildfires are increasing and that the wildfire season is getting longer in the US. In terms of forest fires over a thousand acres in size, in the 1980s, there were 140. In the 1990s, there were 160. And from 2000 to 2012, there were 250. And as already mentioned, 2017 was California's worst wildfire season . . . until 2018.[4]

So if they're not willing to talk about the obvious causes of our pop-up infernos, what was NBC Nightly News reporting on? Well, they spent a good amount of time on the firefighters—correctly informing viewers that these men and women are heroes putting their lives on the line to try to save people they've never met. Good job, NBC. You only missed one thing. You somehow failed to say that many of the firefighters you highlighted are *prisoners locked away in California's correctional system!*

Estimates are that 30 percent of the state's firefighters are prisoners, and it's clear from the uniforms that many of those NBC filmed were indeed inmates.[5] Sure, they volunteered for that job, but many of them are locked up for small crimes and see no way out of the misery and hardship of prison other than to "volunteer" for fire duty. It's kind of like how I "volunteered" to give my wallet and shoes to that guy with a gun when he casually noted that he liked my wallet and shoes.

Furthermore, the inmates are working as firefighters for roughly one dollar per hour.[6]

One dollar per hour.

They get paid less than the amount of money most people are willing to bend down to pick up if they see it in a puddle. But *none* of this is said by NBC *Nightly News*, even as they show video of the inmates fighting fires. This would be like showing Nike sweatshop workers in Indonesia and saying, "These fine craftsmen are making your shoes. Oh man, do they love making shoes. They volunteered to do it."

Are you starting to get the point? Kate Snow's job—like most of those in mainstream media—is to cover up your reality. Her job is to make you think we live in a system that can recover from this carnage *without* large-scale changes, without a new economic paradigm that doesn't reward waste and planned obsolescence and profiting off the lives of others. Generally speaking, the job of mainstream corporate outlets is to ignore the harsh reality that our endless consumption and furious appetite for fossil fuels are burning our country, turning it into a desert wasteland—and the easiest response is to throw slave labor at the problem.

On the other hand, it's the job of you and me to see through the propaganda, through the spectacle and the bullshit, and to fight for a better world.

Maybe it will help if I predict that 20 years from now we all will have woken up from this mass delusion and switched to a sustainable, green, egalitarian economic system.

It's about time I had a positive prediction come true.

NOTES

1 Staff and agencies, "Trump Blames California Wildfires on Forest Mismanagement Again," *Guardian*, November 16, 2018, accessed September 25, 2019, https://www.theguardian.com/us-news/2018/nov/16/trump-california-wildfires-forest-management.

2 Antonia Blumberg and Sarah Ruiz-Grossman, "California's Wildfires This Year Have Been Breaking Records," HuffPost, December 9, 2017, accessed September 25, 2019, https://www.huffingtonpost.com/entry/california-wildfires-breaking-records_us_5a2b0e69e4b069ec48ad6d11.

3 Ted MacDonald, "National Broadcast TV News Mentioned Climate Change in Less than 4 Percent of California Wildfire Coverage," Media Matters for America, November 16, 2018, accessed September 25, 2019, https://www.mediamatters.org/blog/2018/11/16/National-broadcast-TV-news-mentioned-climate-change-in-less-than-4-percent-of-California-w/222097.

4 "Is Global Warming Fueling Increased Wildfire Risks?" Union of Concerned Scientists, last revised July 24, 2018, accessed September 25, 2019, https://www.ucsusa.org/global-warming/science-and-impacts/impacts/global-warming-and-wildfire.html#.W_H2hmRKjog.

5 Julia Lurie, "30 Percent of California's Forest Firefighters Are Prisoners," *Mother Jones*, August 14, 2015, accessed September 25, 2019, https://www.motherjones.com/environment/2015/08/40-percent-californias-fires-are-fought-prison-inmates/.

6 Daniele Selby, "California Is on Fire: These Inmates Are Putting Out Flames for Just $1 an Hour," Global Citizen, October 12, 2017, accessed September 25, 2019, https://www.globalcitizen.org/en/content/inmates-wildfire-california-firefighters-prison-la/.

WE HAVE LESS THAN A SECOND LEFT

None of us should be thinking about anything other than climate change. We all kind of know it, even if we think we don't know it. Even people who deny climate change exists probably secretly know it.[1] They're just confusing what they *want* to be true with what they subconsciously *know* to be true. I did the same thing when I was a child and tennis legend Jimmy Connors lost in the semifinals of the 1991 US Open after his monumental run at the ancient age of 39. (To an 11-year-old, 39 sounds pretty close to mummified.) I was certain Jimmy would be playing in the finals. I knew deep within my bones that Jimbo would dazzle us with diving volleys and mid-court passing shots in the championship match, because how could the powers that be allow the only character America genuinely cared about to bow out before the finals? In my mind it was akin to killing off Iron Man halfway through the movie *Iron Man*.

Jimmy Connors did not show up to the finals. Climate change is the only thing we should be thinking about.

You see, the planet we call home has existed for roughly 4.55 billion years. But numbers that large mean almost nothing to me or to most people, so I choose to break it down. If we lay the age of the earth out over a calendar year, that would amount to 518,264 years per hour or 144 years per second. So if we have 10 or 11 years until the point of no return, as climate scientists have repeatedly told us, that means we have less than a decisecond left before midnight in which to change our society completely to avoid turning the Earth into a piping hot fajita.[2] (If you want to be more generous and instead look at how long modern Homo sapiens have been walking around, it's 315 thousand years. So if you lay that over a calendar year, we have roughly 15 minutes before the stroke of midnight to combat climate change. Not sure that makes me feel much better.)

I don't just mean there should be a report every couple hours about climate change by our bloviating bullhorns of mainstream news. I don't mean once a day you should mention to a friend that Al Gore seems vaguely douchey but probably has a point. I mean climate change should be *all* we're thinking about. It should be a major factor in every conversation, every job, every TV show, every humor column, every tweet, every clever T-shirt slogan, and every fortune cookie message. Climate change should be everything.

Plastic action figures for kids should have one arm melted off to symbolize the effects of climate change. Your server at a nice restaurant should sprinkle sand in your soup du jour to remind you of the disappearance of fresh water. Ice cream should be exclusively served melted to symbolize rising temperatures. Hamburgers should cost 200 dollars to compensate for the global emissions of factory farming. And every time you go ice skating someone should punch you in the face and yell, "Enjoy it while it lasts!"

We have less than a second left.

Simply put, humans have no business going about our day-to-day activities as if we aren't on the event horizon. It's equivalent to working on your model train set while your kitchen is burning down, your spouse is in the bathroom battling an alligator that's taken up residence in the bathtub, and your 12-year-old daughter is in the living room, having just been offered heroin for the first time. Right now, humanity is still focused on the model train.

The International Governmental Panel on Climate Change says the point of no return is the year 2030.[3] This obviously doesn't mean everything will spontaneously combust at the stroke of midnight 2030 (although that would be fascinating to watch). It means that after that point—if we're not living vastly different lives—no effort will stop the planet from becoming uninhabitable, and we humans inevitably will go extinct, and there inevitably will be no more skiing (both due to a lack of snow and due to a lack of fleshy beings to ride on skis). The year 2030 is the point of no return. It is the date of our impending, prolonged suicide.

Let's assume the world's greatest climate scientists are *way off*. Let's assume these people who do nothing other than study climatic models using computer programs so sophisticated I wouldn't be qualified to turn them on—let's assume they have their swollen heads up their highly educated asses. Let's assume that they were *so wrong* that it's not 10 years but, instead, 20 years until the point of no return, so the amount of time we have left is double what they thought. That still means we should be thinking about nothing other than climate change. It still means our very survival as a species, or lack thereof, will be decided in the next couple of decades. It still means we have only a second.

Maybe we're right to die off. Maybe our hubris and egos the size of SUVs have doomed us, and we should just give up and enjoy our final few years. But if that's the case, I would like an announcement. I would honestly prefer a national address by some of our so-called leaders stating clearly, "Look, folks, to continue civilized society of the human species, we would need to change everything. Every single one of us would have to labor toward a massive shift to a sustainable culture that works in harmony with nature rather than abusing nature like it's a servant who gave us an ugly look. We would have to focus on achieving this new society rather than spending a third of our free time watching superhero movies. But we have no intention of doing that because it sounds kinda hard, not to mention that corporate profits would suffer in the short term. So instead, we're declaring here and now that we'll all just keep functioning as is until such time as the oceans turn to acid, the ever-growing storms consume us, and California feels like the inside of a kiln. According to our best minds, that will be 10 to 20 years from now, so don't worry about starting that retirement fund. Don't buy the extended warranty on that vacuum. And whatever you do, at no point and under no circumstances should you quit smoking and drinking. . . . Thank you, and good night."

If that's the choice we've decided to make, then I want an announcement along these lines. On the other hand, if we decide to do the opposite and save ourselves, someone should probably let everyone know it's an "all hands on deck" scenario.

Let's make the call. We have less than a second left.

NOTES

1   Oliver Milman and Fiona Harvey, "US Is Hotbed of Climate Change Denial, Major Global Survey Finds," *Guardian*, May 7, 2019, accessed September 25, 2019, https://www.theguardian.com/environment/2019/may/07/us-hotbed-climate-change-denial-international-poll.

2   "World 'Nearing Critical Point of No Return' on Climate Change, Delegate Warns, as Second Committee Debates Sustainable Development," United Nations Meetings Coverage and Press Releases, October 15, 2018, accessed September 25, 2019, https://www.un.org/press/en/2018/gaef3500.doc.htm.

3   Brandon Miller and Jay Croft, "Planet Has Only until 2030 to Stem Catastrophic Climate Change, Experts Warn," CNN, October 8, 2018, accessed September 28, 2019, https://www.cnn.com/2018/10/07/world/climate-change-new-ipcc-report-wxc/index.html.

WALL STREET IS THE DEFINITION OF A PONZI SCHEME (LITERALLY)

Maybe it makes me unsophisticated, but I don't think about the stock market that much. I know that many say it's the central nervous system of our economy. I know its estimated worth is around 30 trillion dollars.[1] And I know that when it tanks, the lives of millions of Americans are wrecked, ruined, and upended. I know that when that happens, the powerful millionaires (and billionaires) who caused said destruction generally grab their money and their well-coiffed dogs and run for it. (Sometimes our government has to step in to make sure the elites get *all* of their money and don't have to share in the devastation they've dispensed to the lower classes.)

But, in my day-to-day life, I don't think much about the stock market. So maybe I shouldn't care that the entire thing is a gigantic fraud. But I do. I do care. And you should too.

In a few minutes' time you will see that our stock market is a Ponzi scheme. (And, unfortunately, it doesn't matter whether you're happy or sad or ambivalent about that fact. It will be true nonetheless.)

When you picture buying stock in a company, what do you picture? You probably imagine a company like PepsiCo, and you are an investor in that company. You own a tiny piece of it, and because of that, you get a tiny proportion of the profits, which are called "dividends." Well, that's *not* what a stock is. That's what stocks *used* to be, but that was back when top hats were worn by non-magicians, and if a lady showed her knees in public, she was considered a floozy who should die alone.

In modern times, you almost never receive the profits of the business. Dividends are rarely paid out, and they don't usually amount to much. Plus, the company is not obligated to pay you anything for your stock *ever*.

Don't take it from me, take it from someone much smarter than me. Here's an example about Google from Tan Liu's book *The Ponzi Factor*:

> A share of Google can trade around $900, but Google explicitly states in writing that the par value of their stock is only $0.001. Google also says that they do not pay their investors any dividends, and their class C shareholders have no voting rights. So, if you own a share of GOOG, you won't receive any money from Google, you won't be allowed to vote on corporate issues, and Google isn't obligated to pay you anything more than $0.001 for that share you bought for $900.[2]

So this begs the question, "What the hell do you own?" The gut-wrenching answer is nothing. You own *nothing*. You own a slip of toilet paper that you might be able to convince someone else to pay you for.

Next, if you're feeling cheeky, you might ask, "Then where do the profits come from? If I buy Google at 20 dollars and sell it for 220 dollars, where did that 200 dollars come from?" The answer is it came from other investors who were willing to buy the stock. As Tan Liu puts it, "This is actually a negative-sum situation because the underlying company isn't involved in the transaction. The investors are just cannibalizing each other for profits, and there are fees attached to every transaction."[3]

Ah, cannibalizing each other for profits—now this is starting to sound like an American enterprise! It says it right there on our flag, "America: cannibalizing each other for profits since 1776!"

The money you make from most stocks, if you make money, is coming from other investors pumping new money in. And if there aren't new investors willing to buy your stock, then you're just screwed, standing there with your thumb up your ass (which is an odd expression if it's supposed to mean the person is doing nothing; in fact, it sounds like they're involved in a very significant event).

So, to rehash, this is a system where you buy into something and the only way you make money is by convincing someone else to buy it. If no one does, then you lose everything. Why does that sound familiar? Oh, I know. It's the dictionary definition of a Ponzi scheme.

Again, don't take my word for it. The Securities and Exchange Commission (SEC) defines a Ponzi scheme as "[a]n investment fraud that involves the payment of purported returns to existing investors from funds contributed by new investors."[4]

The stock market is a Ponzi scheme. A Ponzi scheme is the stock market.

Some may argue that a Ponzi scheme usually involves lying to the investor. Yet Wall Street has that in spades as well. Most investors don't understand that they own literally nothing. They don't know that they are simply gambling. And they don't know that their profit relies on everyone still believing the fraud is real.

This means that the only way to get your money back or to profit is to find *another* person willing to buy it. Now, don't get me wrong. Your argument may be, "This is America— there's always another chump! We are based on a long, time-honored tradition of never running out of chumps! We're infested with 'em." That's a fair point, but I don't think you see anyone proudly touting *that* as the definition of the stock market. I would actually respect the whole system if right on the front of the stock exchange it said, "Put your money into the stock market! The only way you'll make more money is if you find a dolt to buy whatever stocks you just bought.

But there are an infinite number of dolts! This gravy train is powered by morons. So you have nothing to worry about."

If it said that on the door of the stock exchange, I would invest.

But the fact that our stock market is a house of cards built on idiocy, stacked on spider webs, hanging tenuously from the Hindenburg, is actually kind of a big deal. Think about this:

> As of Sept. 2017, the NASDAQ and the NY Stock Exchange had a combined value of over $30 trillion. . . . [This] means investors believe they are entitled to $30 trillion in real money. But there is only $1.6 trillion of cash circulating in the US economy, and $3.8 trillion in existence in the entire US economic system.

Only 3.8 trillion dollars in hard cash, which means the stock market is built mostly on nothing (much like Jared Kushner). And if a *fraction* of investors wanted their cash at the same time, it would collapse.

Let me just say, I don't have any problem with gambling. If you want to gamble at a casino, then gamble your little heart out. Stay up all night until you're on your last two dollars trying to give a handie to a slot machine in hopes it might pay ya afterwards. Go for it. But the casinos are honest with you. They tell you it's gambling. The front of a casino doesn't say "Invest your pension in roulette. Do you have a child with a degenerative disease? Then put all your savings on red-32 so that he'll be taken care of after you're gone."

Casinos don't say that. The myth of the stock market does.

And some people may think that if it were truly gambling, that would mean it's not predictable. Yet finance professionals claim they know how to analyze and predict the market. So you put your money in their (greasy) hands, and they help you grow your fortune. Well, multiple tests have been done to see whether the professionals know how to predict the market. Liu referenced one contest that was also covered by *Forbes*: "[The contest] was between amateur students, finance professionals, and a cat named Orlando, who did all his investing by tossing his favorite toy mouse onto an electronic grid. Orlando, the cat, won the competition."[5]

I repeat: A *cat* was able to better predict the stock market. Yet trillions of dollars in pensions and life savings are dumped into stocks by people hoping that whoever they trusted that money to is smarter than a cat.

But they aren't. They aren't smarter than the fucking cat.

What other profession is that true for? Anything from math teacher to maintenance man to tennis player, if you were worse than a cat, they would get rid of the whole profession. (And at some point, someone would say, "Besides, the kitten tennis players draw a far bigger audience anyway.")

But it's true for financial advisers—because the stock market is a Ponzi scheme. It's a racket, a hustle, a con, a fast one, a hose job, a crooked calzone! (I think I made up that last one.)

Yet in many cities gambling is illegal. They'll send in armed police to break up poker games. You have to get a permit for a *raffle*. But when a sociopath in Chicago bets your entire pension and loses, there's no SWAT team, no arrests. Because it's a *legalized* Ponzi scheme.

By the way, these ideas are not allowed on our corporate media or financial websites. The almighty stock market does not permit even the slightest doubt to creep in. Tan Liu has tried to put his ideas on popular finance blogs and web forums, and they are often either deleted or he's been banned altogether. He's been banned from Quora and from editing Wikipedia. They act like he went on a Scientology website and wrote, "You know Tom Cruise is not an alien messiah. He's just a short weirdo!"

It's tough to overstate the impact this con game has on our world and our lives. For example, when the news came out that North Korea had brokered peace with South

Korea, the stocks of the major weapons contractors crashed.[6] Billions of dollars were "lost." That exerts major pressure on powerful people to ensure peace does *not* happen. This is just one example of how strong the gravity of this Ponzi scheme is.

There are some steps we could take to make the stock market less exploitative. We could stop speaking about stocks as if they're money. You know, stop saying you have one thousand dollars of Apple shares and instead say you've got "one thousand padoodles of Apple shares." If you sell them, only then do you have a thousand dollars.

Step two is to realize that the market economy in general is designed to exploit billions of us while a tiny number get ridiculously rich. It doesn't care about the health or sustainability of our society as it facilitates the extraction of all the wealth and resources by sociopaths. Just ask Jeff Bezos—he's now worth 150 *billion* padoodles of Amazon stock, while his workers are on food stamps.

NOTES

1   Vito J. Racanelli, "The U.S. Stock Market Is Now Worth $30 Trillion," Barron's, January 18, 2018, accessed September 25, 2019, https://www.barrons.com/articles/the-u-s-stock-market-is-now-worth-30-trillion-1516285704.

2   Tan Liu, *The Ponzi Factor: The Simple Truth about Investment Profits* (Lewes, DE: QuantStyle, 2017), 8.

3   Ibid., 3.

4   "Fast Answers: Ponzi Schemes," U.S. Securities and Exchange Commission, last revised October 9, 2013, accessed September 25, 2019, https://www.sec.gov/fast-answers/answersponzihtm.html.

5   Frederick E. Allen, "Cat Beats Professionals at Stock Picking," *Forbes*, January 15, 2013, accessed September 25, 2019, https://www.forbes.com/sites/frederickallen/2013/01/15/cat-beats-professionals-at-stock-picking/#3f0ddc76621a.

6   Rachel Blevins, "Military Industrial Complex Stocks Sent Crashing as North and South Korea Achieve Peace," Free Thought Project, April 29, 2018, accessed September 25, 2019, https://thefreethoughtproject.com/lockheed-martin-raytheon-northrop-among-military-stocks-sent-crashing-by-korea-peace-deal/.

GOLDMAN SACHS JUST ADMITTED CURING DISEASES IS BAD FOR BUSINESS

Goldman Sachs has outdone itself this time. That's saying a lot for an investment firm that both helped cause and then exploited a global economic meltdown, increasing its own wealth and power, while helping to boot millions of Americans out of their homes.[1]

But now Goldman Sachs is openly saying in financial reports that curing people of terrible diseases is not good for business.

I wish this were a joke. It sounds like a joke. In fact, I'll show you later that it used to be one of my favorite jokes. But, first, the facts.

In a recent report, a Goldman analyst asked clients: "Is curing patients a sustainable business model?"[2] Salveen Richter wrote:

> The potential to deliver "one-shot cures" is one of the most attractive aspects of gene therapy. . . . However, such treatments offer a very different outlook with regard to recurring revenue versus chronic therapies. . . . While this proposition carries tremendous value for patients and society, it could represent a challenge for genome medicine developers looking for sustained cash flow.[3]

Yes, a Goldman analyst has said outright that curing people will hurt their cash flow. And he said that in a note designed to steer clients away from investing in cures. Can "human progress" have a bottom? Because, if so, this is the bottom of so-called human progress—down where the mud eels mate with the cephalopods. (Or at least that's how I picture the bottom.)

This analyst note is one of the best outright examples I've ever seen of how brutal our market economy is. In the past, this truth would not have been spoken. It would've lived deep within a banker's soul and nowhere else. It would've been viewed as too repulsive for the wealthy elite to say, "We don't want to cure diseases because that will be bad for our wallet. We want people to suffer for as long as possible. Every suffering human enriches us a little bit more."

We're circling the drain in the toilet bowl, and, as you know, the contents speed up as they near the end, the event horizon. We are beginning to see more and more how disgusting a "profit above all else economy" really is. When Donald Trump bombed Syria, the stocks of weapons contractors shot up.[4] That spike in stocks is a spike in the gravity of capitalism, pulling people toward death and destruction. Profit has power. And its power is exerted on the society as a whole.

Furthermore, there is no debate about this on your mainstream outlets. There is no discussion as to whether war profiteering is what we really want out of our society. None. You tell me: How many perfectly coiffed CNN or Fox News hosts stated, "Weapons contractors benefited from our bombing. Isn't that revolting? Doesn't that just make you gag in your soup? Doesn't that mean we've created an upside-down system that rewards barbaric bullshit?"

You will not hear that discussion. You're more likely to hear them discuss the best blind ping pong player to ever star in a short film about self-harm. Hard news topics do not see the light of day on our suffocated corporate airwaves.

And believe it or not, the Goldman note gets even worse. The analyst says, "In the case of infectious diseases such as hepatitis C, curing existing patients also decreases the number of carriers able to transmit the virus to new patients."[5]

Decreases the number of carriers? Goldman Sachs . . . is in a financial partnership . . . with fucking infectious diseases.

Let that sink in. Sit with that and decide whether you want to keep your seat on spaceship Earth. I'll wait.

When I first read about this—after I stopped choking on my tongue—I realized it made more sense than I first thought. I've always felt Lloyd Blankfein had a striking resemblance to Hepatitis C. But it turns out he just *works with* Hepatitis C. They're just really close friends and business partners. (But I heard Ebola is the godfather to his kids.)

Our aggressive strain of unfettered capitalism has blasted beyond satire in many ways. In one of my favorite Chris Rock specials, *Bigger & Blacker*, which I first saw when I was a teenager, he had a joke that blew my mind. He said something like, "They ain't never gonna cure AIDS. They ain't *never* gonna cure AIDS. There's too much money in it. The money's not in the cure. The money's in the comeback! The money's in the comeback."

And I found that bit hilarious. I loved it. Because I thought it was a joke. Now, I see—it ain't no joke. He's goddamn right. They aren't even trying to cure infectious diseases that make them piles of cash. Instead, the moneyed interests are complaining to their clients that they need to avoid curing these diseases. Because not only do they lose money on the patient who no longer needs meds, they also lose money because that patient won't pass the disease onto others.

I swear these drug companies are roughly two weeks away from just going, "Hey, what if we send Bruce—that guy in the copy room—out to stab people in the back of the neck with infected needles? Is that over the line? Because that would increase our cash flow. And not only do we make money from the newly infected person, but they're likely to pass it on to other people. How great is that?"

A profit-driven world creates a disgusting reality with a contorted value system. A world where oil companies view oil spills that destroy whole coastal communities as the price of doing business. In fact, they even declared it's good for the local economy.[6] A world where millions of animals abused for their entire lives is just the price of doing brunch. A world where massive hurricane destruction is a business opportunity rather than a tragedy.[7] "Honey, check the weather report. Are there any 155-mile-per-hour business opportunities ripping through any Caribbean islands?"

And now corporations no longer fret over government interference—because they own the government. For them to worry about that would be like you worrying that your carpet might stop you from going out to a movie this evening. I think we've established what the carpet does. It lays there. Corporations now spew forth their true goals and motivations without much concern for the backlash. They can do things like use attack dogs on protesters at Standing Rock and not worry about the consequences.[8] Who cares? The worst that could happen to them is they pay a fine—a "sorry we bit you with vicious man-eating dogs" fine.

We have a value systems disorder. A large percentage of our society now views this Goldman Sachs-style thinking as acceptable. It should be viewed as just as grotesque as beating someone over the head, and then selling them bandages. Now imagine that's your company's business model. And you get investors to help you achieve it. Next to a glowing PowerPoint presentation you say, "You guys help me pay for the baseball bat. I'll beat people over the head with that bat. My bat-swinging skills are well documented. I then sell the bloodied victims our top-shelf bandages. And with little effort on your part, you get a cut of the profits. It's a rock-solid investment."

That's how we need to view what Goldman Sachs is saying in this analyst note.

The only way a system ends up at this point—with our values this far upside down—is with endless advertising in a profit-driven society. This is a system built on the exploitation of others for gain. There was no time when that was not true. And that's why we need a revolution of the mind.

NOTES

1   Lisa Mayers, Rich Gardella, and John W. Schoen, "No End in Sight to Foreclosure Quagmire," NBCNews.com, September 5, 2011, accessed October 12, 2019, http://www.nbcnews.com/id/42881365/ns/business-personal_finance/t/no-end-sight-foreclosure-quagmire/#.XZqp3tVKHog.

2   Tae Kim, "Goldman Sachs Asks in Biotech Research Report: 'Is Curing Patients a Sustainable Business Model?'" CNBC, April 11, 2018, accessed September 25, 2019, https://www.cnbc.com/2018/04/11/goldman-asks-is-curing-patients-a-sustainable-business-model.html.

3   Beth Mole, "'Is Curing Patients a Sustainable Business Model?' Goldman Sachs Analysts Ask," Ars Technica, April 12, 2018, accessed September 25, 2019, https://arstechnica.com/tech-policy/2018/04/curing-disease-not-a-sustainable-business-model-goldman-sachs-analysts-say/.

4   C.J. Atkins, "Syria Airstrikes Added $10 Billion to Missile Manufacturer Stock Values," People's World, April 16, 2018, accessed September 28, 2019, https://www.peoplesworld.org/article/syria-airstrikes-added-10-billion-to-missile-manufacturer-stock-values/.

5   Kim, "Goldman Sachs Asks in Biotech Research Report: 'Is Curing Patients a Sustainable Business Model?'"

6   David Brennan, "Massive Oil Spill 'Welcome Boost' to Economy, Says BP," *Newsweek*, accessed September 25, 2019, April 6, 2018, http://www.newsweek.com/massive-oil-spill-welcome-boost-economy-says-bp-874650.

7   "'The Battle for Paradise': Naomi Klein on Disaster Capitalism & the Fight for Puerto Rico's Future," Democracy Now! March 21, 2018, accessed September 25, 2019, https://www.democracynow.org/2018/3/21/the_battle_for_paradise_naomi_klein.

8   "Standing Rock Special: Unlicensed #DAPL Guards Attacked Water Protectors with Dogs & Pepper Spray," Democracy Now! November 24, 2016, accessed September 25, 2019, https://www.democracynow.org/2016/11/24/standing_rock_special_unlicensed_dapl_guards.

ONE MAN COULD END WORLD HUNGER, BUT HE WON'T

I do not want to talk about Jeff Bezos.

But in order to not talk about Jeff Bezos, I have to talk about Jeff Bezos.

We all know the Lex Luthor–looking head of Amazon is the richest human in the world. He achieved a net worth of more than 150 billion dollars by selling everything that has ever existed . . . with free shipping.[1] It turns out the only thing stopping the human race from giving all our money to one man was that pesky $4.99 shipping fee. (His net worth is, of course, somewhat lower now following his divorce.)

But let me stop right here. Even the way we talk about economics is influenced by a capitalist culture that tells us amassing money is the answer to everything. Did you notice I said Bezos "achieved" a net worth of 150 billion dollars, and that seems like a normal way to phrase it? However, would you say, "Jeffrey Dahmer achieved eating the hearts of 10 different people?" No, that would sound odd to you. Yet having 150 billion dollars is nearly as sociopathic, and still we use terminology as if it's *great*!

But, like I said, this column is not about Jeff Bezos. It's about clean water.

Clean water is one of the most important things to anyone and everyone (second only to nacho cheese). Yet millions around the world don't have clean water or struggle to get it. A report by the UN "estimated that 300 million people on the continent [of Africa], more than a third of the population, have no fixed supply [of clean water]."[2] And 2.5 billion worldwide lack proper sanitation. The CDC says 2,200 children die a day from diarrheal diseases—mostly from unclean water.[3]

Millions of people in total die each year from a lack of clean water. So how much would it cost to change that? It would cost 10 billion dollars a year to bring pure water to the entire world.[4]

Jeff Bezos himself could provide the world with clean water for the next 15 years.

He could save millions upon millions of lives. But instead of doing that, he will continue to enrich himself by delivering sex toys in a box with a smiley on it.

But this is not about Jeff Bezos. It's about world hunger. According to UNICEF, 22 thousand children die each day due to poverty,[5] while the UN in 2015 estimated it would cost 30 billion dollars a year to end world hunger. Imagine—not a soul hungry![6] And, big shock—when people aren't hungry, there's less crime, less hatred, better decision-making, and so forth. Hunger correlates with all kinds of shitty stuff, which means we all benefit when there's no hunger. Think about it; you probably have coworkers who miss lunch and start spraying hate crimes around the office. Then you have to say, "Leslie, I think if you just had a taco, you would stop using the C-word so much." Now imagine Leslie on a global scale.

Jeff Bezos himself could end world hunger for five straight years. If he teamed up with the Koch brothers, they could do it for eight to 10 years.

But Bezos wouldn't do that. Instead, he'll just make billions convincing people to put Amazon Echo spy systems into their own homes.

This column is not about Jeff Bezos. It's about Flint, Michigan.

You remember how upset we were about Flint's water? It was poisoned with lead. It was destroying lives of people who were already poor to begin with. Then the authorities came to the conclusion it would cost 216 million dollars to fix, and everyone was aghast.[7] That's an insane amount of money. How could *any* city afford that?!

Jeff Bezos could pay to repair Flint's water supply 694 times over.

He could pay for it 690 times over and still have 864 million dollars left to pay for a cast of people to dance around him dressed like wood sprites and sprinkle glitter on his shining bald head for the rest of his fucking life. (So don't say he wouldn't be happy.)

But this column is not about Jeff Bezos. It's about homelessness.

There are 554 thousand homeless people in the US, one of the richest countries in the world.[8] What would it cost to give each of these struggling people his or her own apartment? Recent numbers show the cheapest apartments to rent in America are in Wichita, Kansas (because why would ya . . . unless you were heavily invested in grasshoppers?). In Wichita, an apartment costs 632 dollars per month.[9] (In San Francisco, that's the cost of the monthly utility bill for a dog house.) So 632 dollars per month amounts to 7,584 dollars per year. Therefore, the total cost to give every American houseless person an apartment in Wichita would be 4.2 billion dollars.

Jeff Bezos could give every homeless person their own apartment for the next 36 *years*.

This is one man we're talking about! But Jeff Bezos would never do that. He'd rather push a bag of three thousand live ladybugs on someone actually searching Amazon for *Ladybugs* the Rodney Dangerfield film (which was apparently intended as a children's movie but now seems like a guidebook for how to become a #MeToo predator).[10]

But this column is not about Jeff Bezos. It's about education.

When people go to college without coming out stuck under immense debt, it often changes their whole lives. They can get better jobs, eat healthier, provide for their family. AffordableColleges.com tells us, "According to the American Association of Community Colleges, the average yearly cost of tuition and fees for community college students in the U.S. is $3,347."[11] It usually takes two years to graduate from community college, so the cost for two years is 6,694 dollars.

Jeff Bezos could pay for the entire community college education of 22.4 million students.

That's more than the entire number of college students enrolled this year across our country. Of course, you'd have to pay for your own beer bongs, posters of John Belushi in the "college" sweater, macaroni stuck to the floor, and pregnancy tests. (But I know a guy who can get you a homemade pregnancy test for 35 cents. It's made out of alkaline batteries and sawdust, but it'll spot a freakin' baby a mile away.)

However, this column is not about Jeff Bezos. It's about the system that *created* Bezos.

If you removed Bezos from Amazon tomorrow and vacuumed all his money away, he would be replaced by another sick hoarder of egregious wealth. This is because we have a deathly ill economic system. Think about it this way—the goals of our economy (and any economy), according to Zeitgeist Movement founder Peter Joseph,[12] and I agree, *should* be:

- pursuit of abundance (all people's basic needs are met);
- sustainability (can the system keep going forever);
- liberation of humanity from hard and dangerous labor (nobody doing jobs they hate);
- adaptation to emerging technologies and variables.

Makes sense—we should seek a sustainable system where nobody is dying or miserable. Here's the problem—unfettered capitalism doesn't even claim to be *attempting* any of that. Our economy's mission statement is basically to "preserve inefficiency for the sake of monetary circulation, economic growth and power preservation."[13]

Profit over all else. It doesn't matter how many people die or work at an Amazon warehouse for pennies. Does. Not. Matter. So it's not that capitalism is failing in this new Gilded Age. Rather, capitalism is *succeeding* at what it was meant to do: amass all the money in a tiny number of hands and exploit everyone else.

That's what this column is about.

NOTES

1   Paul R. La Monica, "Happy Prime Day! Bezos Worth $150 Billion as Amazon Hits All-Time High," CNN, July 16, 2018, accessed September 25, 2019, https://money.cnn.com/2018/07/16/technology/amazon-stock-prime-day-jeff-bezos-net-worth/index.html.

2   Associated Press, "Price of Safe Water for All: $10 Billion and the Will to Provide It," *New York Times*, November 23, 2000, accessed September 25, 2019, https://www.nytimes.com/2000/11/23/world/price-of-safe-water-for-all-10-billion-and-the-will-to-provide-it.html.

3   "Global Water, Sanitation, & Hygiene (WASH): Global WASH Fast Facts," Centers for Disease Control and Prevention, last revised April 11, 2016, accessed September 25, 2019, https://www.cdc.gov/healthywater/global/wash_statistics.html.

4   Associated Press, "Price of Safe Water for All."

5   "11 Facts about Global Poverty," DoSomething.org, accessed September 25, 2019, https://www.dosomething.org/us/facts/11-facts-about-global-poverty.

6   "The Cost to End World Hunger," Borgen Project, February 15, 2015, accessed September 25, 2019, https://borgenproject.org/the-cost-to-end-world-hunger/.

7   Ryan Felton, "Fixing Flint's Contaminated Water System Could Cost $216m, Report Says," *Guardian*, June 6, 2016, accessed September, 2019, https://www.theguardian.com/us-news/2016/jun/06/flint-water-crisis-lead-pipes-infrastructure-cost.

8   "US Homeless People Numbers Rise for First Time in Seven Years," BBC, December 6, 2017, accessed September 25, 2019, https://www.bbc.com/news/world-us-canada-42248999.

9   Amber C. Snider, "What American Millennials Should Know before Renting an Apartment," Culture Trip, January 3, 2018, accessed

September 25, 2019, https://theculturetrip.com/north-america/usa/articles/highest-lowest-rents-u-s-2018/.

10   "Double Order 3000 Live Lady Bugs," Amazon, accessed September 25, 2019, https://www.amazon.com/Double-Order-3000-Ladybugs-Packs/dp/B073RTTK4B.

11   "50 Most Affordable Community Colleges," AffordableColleges.com, accessed September 25, 2019, https://www.affordablecolleges.com/rankings/community-colleges/.

12   TZM Lecture Team, *The Zeitgeist Movement Defined*, January 2014, accessed October 12, 2019, https://www3.thezeitgeistmovement.com/wp-content/uploads/2017/10/The_Zeitgeist_Movement_Defined_PDF_Final.pdf.

13   Ibid.

THE SILVER BULLET TO STOP THE CORPORATE STATE PILLAGE

Every year a certain number of our soldiers decide they'd rather not be involved in shooting people they don't know so that ExxonMobil can have more oil or Lockheed Martin can make more cash or MSNBC/Fox News can give their hosts topics for their upcoming poetry books. Basically, these soldiers do something horrifying, something terrible, something often called "treasonous." . . . They—wait for it—*think for themselves!*

(Glass shatters. Woman screams. Baby cries.)

Nothing is more frightening for our endless war machine than a military grunt who thinks for him or herself. They're supposed to do nothing more than follow orders. They're supposed to ask a superior officer for permission to wear a different color pair of socks. That's right—the biggest, toughest gladiators in our society have to get authorization to switch from boxers to briefs.

I'll get to what this has to do with our inverted totalitarian corporate pillaging in a moment.

One of the more notable soldiers who stood up this year was Spenser Rapone—a second lieutenant discharged on June 18, 2018, for disparaging the US war machine online and promoting a socialist revolution. (Clearly our enormous globe-spanning military complex can obliterate any possible enemies except independent thought, which promptly turns it to a mush akin to pea soup.) Apparently reading about the true story of Pat Tillman pushed Rapone toward the realization that he was a pawn in the middle of a massive lie.[1]

"Pat Tillman showed me I could resist the indoctrination," Rapone said. "I did not have to let the military dehumanize me and turn me into something monstrous. When I learned how his death was covered up to sell the war, it was shocking."[2]

To *sell* the war. Why is it they would need to *sell* a war? Oh, I know—because it's completely unjustifiable. For activities people naturally agree with or enjoy, you don't have to advertise them. Like you don't see ads saying, "Hey, feed your kids. . . . Don't forget." Or a commercial saying, "Try having sex some time. It's fun!" That stuff comes pretty naturally. But you *do* need promotion (read: media propaganda) for our endless war games, because it does *not* come naturally to most of us. War comes naturally to sociopaths, and then it's *sold* to the rest of us, much like a used car or an ill-advised timeshare in Cleveland.

But the military is not the only place where conscientious objectors play a role. It might be the only one where walking away can get you locked up in *prison* spending your days sewing McDonald's uniforms, but there are a lot of moments in our messed-up world when you can turn your back and do the right thing.[3]

For example, fewer and fewer people are willing to do the job of killing millions of animals every year. A recent report "revealed that staff shortages at slaughterhouses [in the U.K. were] threatening Christmas sales. Some 10 thousand positions are unfilled at major abattoirs. . . . The report explains that for most potential applicants, the industry's low pay is not the problem but that 'people simply do not want to do this work anymore.'"[4]

Oh, come on, you fragile snowflakes! "Ewww, I can't handle chopping the heads off a thousand pigs a day. It *hurts my feelings* to end the life of hundreds of sentient beings who haven't done anything to me to warrant such treatment. *Weh!*

I *don't like* loading buckets of adorable chickadees into the grinding colander so they can be turned into a meat milkshake that will ultimately be served to a labradoodle or a puggle. *Boo hoo hoo!*" (I might have made up the term "grinding colander.")

In all seriousness, working at the killing fields of a factory farm has lifelong impacts that no one talks about. (And by "no one," I mean the media and our politicians and most everybody else.) As the *Guardian* reported, "Slaughterhouse work has been linked to a variety of disorders, including post-traumatic stress disorder and perpetration-induced traumatic stress. One pig slaughterer said the 'worst thing' about the work is its 'emotional toll'. . . . A worker at a chicken plant said one of his colleagues was 'hauled off to the mental hospital' after he 'kept having nightmares that chickens were after him.'"[5] (It's tough to say what the chickens would've done with him had they caught him. Professional torture is made difficult by a lack of hands.)

These workers who have walked off the killing floors should be honored as conscientious objectors. They should be rewarded for realizing it's better to get paid to hand out coffees at the coffeehouse than death sentences at the slaughterhouse.

And conscientious objection happens in the big tech world too. This past May, a dozen Google employees quit to protest the company's role in drone-killing technology created for the Pentagon, and another four thousand signed an internal petition to stop the partnership.[6]

While I agree with those who quit, I think if I had worked there, I would've stayed. I would've stayed just so I could stealthily stick into each drone targeting system one of my beard hairs. I could have quietly fucked up the Pentagon's drones for *decades* to come.

There have been many great objectors in our police forces too. Captain Ray Lewis was in the Philadelphia police force for 23 years.[7] Then he became an outspoken critic of police abuse, militarization, excess force, and the inequality that have hollowed out our society like an aggressive virus. He shows up to protests in full uniform and stands on the front lines to help remind the other cops what they should be protecting—and it's not oil pipelines or Wall Street banks. Perhaps most importantly, he does it all with a mustache that looks like it houses squirrels in the winter. It's quite possible that without the facial hair, not a single police officer would give a shit. However, you can really reach a cop through his 'stache. (Sorry, his or her 'stache.)

Conscientious objectors even show up in the grand hallways of the famously lockstep mainstream media outlets. Just last week, veteran national security journalist William Arkin left his job at NBC and MSNBC and basically blasted them in an open letter "for becoming captive and subservient to the national security state, reflexively pro-war . . . and now the prime propaganda instrument of the War Machine's promotion of militarism and imperialism."[8] Of course, anyone who regularly reads independent outlets like Truthdig would probably say Mr. Arkin is roughly 30 years late to this realization. Yet it still takes nerve, gonads, and a spine to turn against your employer, calling them out for manufacturing consent for hundreds of thousands of innocent deaths. (Certain types of deepwater fish are made up of only nerves, gonads, and a spine, and they're constantly being insolent to their employers.)

The truth is, we the people may not have that much power. We don't control our democracy anymore, now that every decision is based on money. We can't instantly change the entire system. But we have one very powerful tool—we have the power of our labor.

Millions of Americans and hundreds of millions worldwide work for corporations or organizations that do evil every single day. This list includes:

- people at the big banks that fund the destruction of our world

- officials sent to steal children from their mothers and fathers
- people working at big oil companies, pushing papers, while knowing we only have 11 years left to completely change our behavior[9]
- soldiers told to drone bomb a guy they've never met before
- merchants in charge of selling Kid Rock T-shirts.

The list is endless, and *all* of these people have the ability to say "I object. I will not help with your villainy."

If they all objected—we would see a different world overnight.

NOTES

1   Kevin Tillman, "After Pat's Birthday," Truthdig, May 27, 2019, accessed September 25, 2019, https://www.truthdig.com/articles/after-pats-birthday-2/.

2   Chris Hedges, "The Soldier's Tale," Truthdig, June 24, 2018, accessed September 25, 2019, https://www.truthdig.com/articles/the-soldiers-tale/.

3   Mark Maxey, "Corporations and Governments Collude in Prison Slavery Racket," People's World, February 7, 2018, accessed September 26, 2019, https://www.peoplesworld.org/article/corporations-and-governments-collude-in-prison-slavery-racket/.

4   Chas Newkey-Burden, "There's a Christmas Crisis Going On: No One Wants to Kill Your Dinner," *Guardian*, November 19, 2018, accessed September 26, 2019, https://www.theguardian.com/commentisfree/2018/nov/19/christmas-crisis-kill-dinner-work-abattoir-industry-psychological-physical-damage.

5   Ibid.

6   Maya Kosoff, "Google Employees Quit to Protest Company's Role in Killing Machines," *Vanity Fair*, May 14, 2018, accessed September 26, 2019, https://www.vanityfair.com/news/2018/05/google-employees-quit-to-protest-companys-role-in-killing-machines.

7   Adam Lidgett, "Former Philadelphia Police Officer Ray Lewis, Arrested during Occupy Protests, Set to Appear at Cleveland Tamir Rice Rally," International Business Times, January 6, 2016, accessed September 26, 2019, https://www.ibtimes.com/former-philadelphia-police-officer-ray-lewis-arrested-during-occupy-protests-set-2252914.

8   Glenn Greenwald, "Veteran NBC/MSNBC Journalist Blasts the Network for Being Captive to the National Security State and Reflexively Pro-War to Stop Trump," Intercept, January 3, 2019, accessed September 26, 2019, https://theintercept.com/2019/01/03/veteran-nbcmsnbc-journalist-blasts-the-network-for-being-captive-to-the-national-security-state-and-reflexively-pro-war-to-stop-trump/.

9   Arthur Neslen, "By 2030, We Will Pass the Point Where We Can't Stop Runaway Climate Change," HuffPost, September 5, 2018, accessed September 26, 2019, https://www.huffingtonpost.com/entry/runaway-climate-change-2030-report_us_5b8ecba3e4b0162f4727a09f.

A GOOD DAY ON WALL STREET IS A BAD DAY FOR MOST AMERICANS

The stock market recently had one of its worst single-day plunges in history: 1,600 points at one point. All the corporate media heads ran around telling you everything will be okay and not to panic because your bichon frisé puppy still will be able to afford his mani-pedi. But the mainstream media are careful to avoid telling you the censored side of this story.

They're not telling you that we have an economy that, at its core, is based on death, misery, and hardship. It's not based on health and happiness and life. When it's humming along, our obliteration of the planet is running full steam ahead, and average workers are being appropriately repressed and held down, hoping to collect enough food stamps to papier-mâché a cast on their broken arm since they can't afford healthcare. In fact, the *Washington Post* admitted it this week—but acted surprised: "Many analysts pointed to a seemingly unusual cause for the turbulence: rising wages."[1]

No, it's not an "unusual" cause at all. When we start doing better—when wages start going up–Wall Streeters shit themselves. This is the norm. They only celebrate when we're fucked, when workers don't have the ability to demand better wages, better treatment, health care, coffee breaks, and less handsy bosses. Stock markets around the world panic when the workers are strong. The stock market is not for us.

According to *Time* magazine, "The Richest 10% of Americans Now Own 84% of All Stocks."[2] We're told we should all celebrate how well the market is doing, but it's just the rich further enriching themselves by playing games with the lives of everyone else. It's like Monopoly, except we regular people are the players—doing the grunt work, going straight to jail, working on the Pennsylvania Railroad all day, and only coming home to a thimble full of soup. The rich are the giant human hands that come down to grab all the money and flick your house off the board.

Over the past year, as the Dow broke 24,000, 25,000, and then 26,000, all the news anchors had on party hats, rubbing their nipples on prime time. Donald Trump tweeted: "Dow rises 5,000 points on the year for the first time ever—Make America great again!" But it wasn't a rally for us. It wasn't a rally for the planet or the animals. It was only a rally for the parasites at the top. The regular humans work their asses off, and the viruses are the ones reaping the benefits—and not even paying their taxes.

I'm pretty sure I've mixed my metaphors, but, still, I think viruses should pay taxes. And tapeworms should have jury duty too.

You want more proof? A leaked 2005 internal Citigroup memo, the parent company of Citibank, read: "The world is dividing into two blocs—the Plutonomy and the rest. . . . Plutonomies [are] economies powered by the wealthy."[3] Ajay Kapur, lead author of the report, said *powered by the wealthy*, but he meant *exploited by the wealthy*. The memo continued: "In a plutonomy there is no such animal as 'the U.S. consumer' or 'the UK consumer,' or indeed the 'Russian consumer.' There are rich consumers, few in number, but disproportionate in the gigantic slice of income and consumption they take. There are the rest, the 'non-rich', the multitudinous many, but only accounting for surprisingly small bites of the national pie."

In 2006, "The Plutonomy Symposium—Rising Tides Lifting Yachts," another internal memo from Citigroup read:

"We should worry less about what the average consumer . . . is going to do, when that consumer is (we think) less relevant to the aggregate data than how the wealthy feel and what they're doing. This is simply a case of mathematics, not morality."[4]

There you go: the rich matter, the non-rich don't matter. Morality matters to them as much as having skid marks on their underwear. They throw it out and never think about it again.

And then the 2005 memo puts the nail in the coffin: "The three levers governments and societies could pull on to end plutonomy are benign. Property rights are generally still intact, taxation policies neutral to favorable, and globalization is keeping the supply of labor in surplus, acting as a brake on wage inflation."

Citigroup is saying that the levers of the state cannot stop us, the rich, from doing whatever we want, because we *own* the government. They're our gimps on a chain in the basement. In case you've forgotten, WikiLeaks emails revealed that Citigroup chose nearly all of Barack Obama's 2008 cabinet.[5] They told him exactly whom to pick before he even became president. And Trump also has surrounded himself with Citigroup and Goldman Sachs affiliates. Makes you wonder if Citigroup could have tested out its power and been like, "For secretary of Housing and Urban Development, we need you to choose Carrot Top. Sorry, yeah, it has to be Carrot Top. That's all we'll accept." And then that night, they're all giggling to themselves in a boardroom in New York: "Oh, my god. He did it. What an idiot."

Right about now, you're thinking, "But, Lee, when the stock market goes down, it hurts productivity. It hurts the GDP." Well, first of all, average Americans are not benefiting from the productivity gains. In 1968, the minimum wage was $1.60. According to the Center for Economic and Policy Research, "If the minimum wage had continued to move with average productivity after 1968, it would have reached $21.72 per hour in 2012. . . . If minimum-wage workers received only half of the productivity gains over the period, the federal minimum would be $15.34."[6]

According to the Economic Policy Institute, "In 2007, average annual incomes of the top 1 percent of households were 42 times greater than incomes of the bottom 90 percent (up from 14 times greater in 1979), and incomes of the 0.1 percent were 220 times greater (up from 47 times greater in 1979)."[7]

Workers' lives didn't get better with productivity. Wall Street steals more and more of the money and gives less and less to the worker. The bottom 90 percent then fight over the scraps and hate each other for it. "Hey! Why do teachers get to have health care, while the rest of us don't? Fuck you, teachers! What have you ever done for society? I'm voting for whoever is taking the health care away from the teachers."

The gains. Go. To. The. Top.

While the stock market has soared, 41.2 million Americans are food insecure, meaning they are forced to skip meals or eat less at meals, and that includes 12.9 million children. How can anyone say we are a successful country while an eighth of our population is food insecure? Sounds to me like you don't know what words mean.

How do we rate success? We look at gross domestic product—how much we're producing. GDP doesn't measure how many kids are drinking toxic water or breathing toxic air. It doesn't measure how many dolphins are choking on plastic beer rings. It only measures how many beers you chug down. It doesn't measure how many trees were planted. It measures how many trees we cut down to make the cardboard for coffee cups and condom boxes. It doesn't rate how screwed the environment is, just how much stuff we buy to keep screwing. Buy a dildo? Good for the economy. Throw an old dildo out? Ends up in the ocean, gets stuck in a whale's blowhole. GDP doesn't care.

In China, the government builds "ghost cities"—massive cities where no one lives, because the act of building them is good for GDP.[8] Of course, it's disastrous for the environment, but who cares? It's good for GDP. GDP doesn't measure how many animals went extinct. It only measures how many animals we ate or sold. You could be eating a bald eagle roasted with giraffe bacon wrapped around it. As long as you bought it at the store, it's good for GDP. And besides the fact that our factory farms are basically government-subsidized pig and cow concentration camps, animal agriculture is the number one cause of greenhouse gases. More than cars. So the number one thing you could do for the planet would be to eat less meat.

Recently a pledge to eat less meat was signed by half a million people.[9] It doesn't even say no meat. It just says, "Take a breather. Slow down a little. Let the last ham hock get all the way down your throat before you stuff the next one in. Give it a second." GDP is a measurement of destruction in a system that demands infinite growth on a planet with finite resources. Gross domestic product: we are the product, and it's gross.

One country does it differently: Bhutan. It measures Gross National Happiness.[10] I agree that that sounds like something singer Meghan Trainor would call her new tour, with opening act the Wiggles. But, still, it's not a bad idea. Gross Domestic Happiness makes sense. If we're not trying to get happiness and sustainability for the most people, then what are we doing? Isn't that supposed to be the point of this ridiculous existence on this tiny spark of galactic light? Anything's better than just measuring production and consumption. Gross Domestic Comfort, Gross Domestic Orgasms, Gross Domestic Roof Over Your Head, Gross Domestic Dude Not Working Two Jobs and Never Seeing His Kids and Can't Afford a Movie Popcorn Without Putting His Daughter Up as Collateral. Any of those would measure our society better than gross domestic product.

I mean, if that's not the point, just let me know, and I'll get on board. *Oh, the point is to make sure a tiny number of individuals can afford to purchase their own islands with helicopter landing pads?*

Oh, I had no idea that was the meaning of life. I'm sorry I've been resisting it so long. In that case, the stock market seems to be working perfectly.

Ecologically, our economy is killing the planet. That's not up for debate. Imagine the aliens that come down here after we've eaten everything, killed everything, and turned it all to dust. Imagine them showing up and going, "What happened to those little fellows that used to be here?"

"Well, they imagined something called the stock market, where nonliving entities called corporations compete to see which one can exploit the earth the most. It eventually swallowed up the whole biosphere they lived in."

"Oh, which corporation won?"

"Ironically, the one called Amazon, which used to be the name of the largest river in the world, until they paved it."

Here's the thing: the stock market is life-blind. It's also death-blind. It's misery- and starvation- and destruction-blind. It doesn't see people or happiness or art or beauty. It sees only profit, which means it is a cancer of our system of values. It's like a guy driving a car and only seeing speed, being completely blind to how many people he runs down. He'd get to his destination in record time and say to the townspeople, who all had family members run over by this maniac, "We did it. I got here in record time. We should all celebrate together."

One percent of America is celebrating. It's time to do things differently.

NOTES

1   Thomas Heath and Heather Long, "Dow Closes Down Nearly 1200 Points in Volatile Trading," *Washington Post*, February 5, 2018, accessed September 26, 2019, https://www.washingtonpost.com/business/economy/dow-drops-more-than-300-at-opening-extending-fridays-losses/2018/02/05/624f72c6-0a80-11e8-8890-372e2047c935_story.html?utm_term=.73cebf79809c.

2   Rob Wile, "The Richest 10% of Americans Now Own 84% of All Stocks," Money, December 19, 2017, accessed September 26, 2019, http://time.com/money/5054009/stock-ownership-10-percent-richest/.

3   Citigroup, "Plutonomy: Buying Luxury, Explaining Global Imbalances" (memo), October 16, 2005, accessed September 26, 2019, https://delong.typepad.com/plutonomy-1.pdf; "The Citigroup Plutonomy Memos: Two Bombshell Documents That Citigroup's Lawyers Try to Suppress, Describing in Detail the Rule of the First 1%," Politicalgates, December 10, 2011, accessed September 26, 2019, https://politicalgates.blogspot.com/2011/12/citigroup-plutonomy-memos-two-bombshell.html; Matthew Yglesias, "The Economics of Plutonomy," Slate, November 21, 2011, accessed September 26, 2019, http://www.slate.com/blogs/moneybox/2011/11/21/the_economics_of_plutonomy.html.

4   TZM Lecture Team, *The Zeitgeist Movement Defined: Realizing a New Train of Thought* (January 2014), accessed September 26, 2019, http://www.nommeraadio.ee/meedia/pdf/RRS/The%20Zeitgeist%20Movement%20Defined.pdf.

5   Tom Eley, "Citigroup Chose Obama's 2008 Cabinet, WikiLeaks Document Reveals," World Socialist Web Site, October 15, 2016, accessed September 26, 2019, https://www.wsws.org/en/articles/2016/10/15/wiki-o15.html.

6   John Schmitt, "The Minimum Wage Is Too Damn Low," Center for Economic and Policy Research, March 2012, accessed September 26, 2019, http://cepr.net/documents/publications/min-wage1-2012-03.pdf.

7   Natalie Sabadish and Lawrence Mishel, "CEO Pay and the Top 1%: How Executive Compensation and Financial-Sector Pay Have Fueled Income Inequality," Economic Policy Institute, May 2, 2012, accessed September 26, 2019, http://www.epi.org/publication/ib331-ceo-pay-top-1-percent/.

8   Laura Mallonee, "The Unreal, Eerie Emptiness of China's 'Ghost Cities,'" *Wired*, February 4, 2016, accessed September 26, 2019, https://www.wired.com/2016/02/kai-caemmerer-unborn-cities/.

9   "Avaaz Sends 'Global Meat Pledge' Email to 46 Million People," Plant-Based News, January 26, 2018, accessed September 26, 2019, https://www.plantbasednews.org/post/avaazglobal-meat-pledge-46-million-people.

10 Kai Schultz, "In Bhutan, Happiness Index as Gauge for Social Ills," *New York Times*, January 17, 2017, accessed September 26, 2019, https://www.nytimes.com/2017/01/17/world/asia/bhutan-gross-national-happiness-indicator-.html.

THE PENTAGON AND MICROSOFT ARE QUIETLY HIJACKING ALL US ELECTIONS

Good news, folks! We have found the answer to the American electoral system!

Why do we need an answer? Well, our electoral system is . . . how do you say . . . a festering rancid corrupt needlessly complex rigged rotten infected putrid pus covered diseased dog pile of stinking dying cockroach filled rat shit smelling like Mitch McConnell under a vat of pig farts. And that's a quote from the *Lancet* medical journal (I think).

But have no fear. The most trustworthy of corporations recently announced they are going to selflessly and patriotically secure our elections. It's a small company run by vegans and powered by love. It goes by the name "Microsoft." (You're forgiven for never having heard of it.)

The recent headlines were grandiose and thrilling:

"Microsoft Offers Software Tools to Secure Elections."[1]
"Microsoft Aims to Modernize and Secure Voting with ElectionGuard."[2]

Could anything be safer than software christened "ElectionGuard™"?! It has "guard" right there in the name. It's as strong and trustworthy as the little-known Crotch Guard™—an *actual oil* meant to be sprayed on one's junk. I'm unclear as to why one sprays it on one's junk, but perhaps it's to secure your erections? (Because they've been microsoft?)

Anyway, Microsoft is foisting their ElectionGuard™ software on us, but worry not that we Americans will be tied down by laborious public debate as to the effectiveness, efficiency, and accountability of said software. According to MintPress, "The election technology is already set to be adopted by half of voting machine manufacturers and some state governments for the 2020 general election."[3] Hardly any public discussion will plague our media or tax our community discourse.

Microsoft describes ElectionGuard™ as "a free open-source software development kit" that "will make voting secure, more accessible, and more efficient anywhere it's used."[4] Wow, those are genuinely great words to hear—free and open-source. The only words I like more than "open-source" are "open bar," but my dream of an open bar at every polling location remains elusive.

MintPress's Whitney Webb recently reported on ElectionGuard™ (much of the information in this column comes from her impressive exposé). She spoke to journalist Yasha Levine, who said, "What open source does is give a veneer of openness that leads one to think that thousands of people have vetted the code and flagged any bugs. But, actually very few people have the time and ability to look at this code. So this idea that open source code is more transparent isn't really true."[5]

And as WikiLeaks proved when they revealed the CIA's Vault 7, whenever the CIA discovers holes in important code, they don't reveal this to the American people.[6] They keep it for themselves to exploit secretly, which is what could be done with ElectionGuard™, resulting in America's continued descent into Banana Republic™ (both senses of the phrase).

So while open-source is better than *not* open-source, it's not a silver bullet. It's like saying that having 90 zombies chasing you is better than 100 zombies chasing you. Sure, but that doesn't mean it's time to sit down and have a cold beer.

The press releases on ElectionGuard™ also touted a dizzying array of election security measures. I've reprinted the list of security measures beginning with the most powerful measure and ending with the least powerful:

1. homomorphic encryption
2. waterproof keyboards.

I imagine some of you are a bit overwhelmed by such an extensive and confusing list. Feel free to take a mental breather now and rejoin this column in a few minutes. Also, I made up number two.

I do acknowledge that "homomorphic encryption" sounds pretty freaking awesome. "Homomorphic" makes you think there might be a gay member of the X-Men. But, in fact, it's a malleable form of encryption, which apparently is not the most secure or most sought-after form of encryption, according to nerds who study the crypto-verse (a term I conjured up just now to sound smarter). I won't get into the details, but the experts seem to agree homomorphic encryption will not turn our elections into an impenetrable wall of democracy, renowned the world over.

On top of that, as Webb stated, "there is an added layer of concern given Microsoft's past, particularly their history of working with US government agencies to bypass encryption."

So the company setting up the encryption for our elections is a company with a résumé of helping the US government break encryption. This is like setting up a system to test for steroids in baseball and asking Sammy Sosa to help you do it.

Yet the Microsoft takeover gets even worse, because it's not only Microsoft. They're doing it in partnership with a cybersecurity firm called Galois. Whitney Webb again:

> Though it describes itself as "a privately held U.S.-owned and -operated company," public records indicate that Galois' only investors are DARPA (the Defense Advanced Research Projects Agency) and the

Office of Naval Research, both of which are divisions of the Department of Defense.[7]

Did you catch that? Galois claims to be a private company but its *only* investor is the *fucking Pentagon*. To rephrase something you already understood in another way so that you get mildly annoyed with me—Microsoft and our war machine are taking over the American electoral system.

Honestly, who would put election software in the hands of DARPA?[8] DARPA's the department that tries to put microchips in soldiers' brains to create Terminators or Robocops or other dystopian hounds of hell. Anything ever invented where your first response upon hearing about it is, "That's fucking awful!" DARPA did that.

I wouldn't even let someone from DARPA look after my cat for the weekend. We all know I'd come home, the cat would have half a head and a GameBoy duct-taped to its ass. "Fuck you, DARPA! I don't care if the Mario Kart theme song plays when it shits. Get out of my apartment!"

Now imagine that scenario but replace the cat with our entire electoral system.

MintPress further revealed Galois has a spin-off company called "Free & Fair" that creates technology for elections and worked with Microsoft to make ElectionGuard. Unfortunately, Free & Fair is connected to every form of neocon think tank, government agency, and large corporation. They're especially in bed with the Department of Homeland Security.

"So what's wrong with that?" you might ask.

As Webb details, "before, during and after the 2016 election, the Department of Homeland Security was caught attempting to hack into state electoral systems in at least three states—Georgia, Indiana, and Idaho—with similar accusations also made by Kentucky and West Virginia. . . . DHS which initially denied it, later responded that the attempted breach was 'legitimate business.'"

Legitimate business? Anytime someone from DHS says they're involved in legitimate business, immediately duck and put your head between your knees.

Plus, the fact that Microsoft wants to introduce this software to us for *free*, should set off an alarm bell the size of Lake Michigan. Microsoft doesn't do *anything* for free. Microsoft doesn't say hello to their grandma for free. They're one of the most powerful companies in America because of their predatory practices. If the Mafia offered you something for free, would you just say "Thanks!" and wander off? Or would you start appreciating your final days with knees that bend?

In this world *free* does not mean *no ulterior motive*. One motive could be to control or rig our entire government. But who would want that? A tiny little country like America? *Please!* Our country is so inconsequential we have a third-rate gameshow host as president.

MintPress may have found another ulterior motive. "Microsoft President Brad Smith announced that the company "'is going to provide the US military with access to the best technology . . . all the technology we create. Full stop.' A month prior to that, Microsoft secured a $480 million contract with the Pentagon to provide the military with its HoloLens technology."[9]

So right after getting hundreds of millions of dollars from our military, Microsoft partners with Pentagon front companies to develop free software to safeguard our elections. It seems clear the real goal is to hand over our elections systems to the military-industrial complex—your friendly neighborhood death machine—and bury the reality of our votes under enough encryption and complex technology that no average citizen really knows what's happening.

Then, if (read: when) an election is rigged with this technology, we won't be able to prove it, because we don't have reliable exit polls anymore.

There's essentially only one remaining exit poll company, Edison Research, and they say outright that they manipulate the exit polls to fit the machine results, which is the *opposite* of a legitimate exit poll. That's the same as a math teacher saying, "I give the kids an algebra test, and when I'm comparing their answers to the correct answers, I adjust their answers to better fit the correct ones." That sounds lovely, but it means you're going to have idiots getting into MIT on fake math scores. If you do it with elections, you have idiots getting into Congress. . . . Won't that be a sad day . . . when Congress is filled with idiots.

Election forensics analyst Jonathan Simon said, "The great irony, and tragedy, here . . . is that we could easily go the opposite direction and quickly solve all the problems of election security if we got the computers out of the process and were willing to invest the modicum of effort needed for humans to count votes observably in public as they once did."[10]

Jonathan Simon, god bless him, has used 55 words to say 11. We could easily fix our fraudulent electoral system, but we won't.

The answer is *not* to hand it over to Microsoft and the Pentagon and the ass clowns who make robotic death machines. The Pentagon can't keep track of 21 *trillion* dollars over the past 20 years—what makes us think they can keep track of hundreds of millions of votes?[11]

The ruling elite have no interest in making sure our voices are heard. They want that as much as they want nunchucks to the balls. If they sought to have our voices heard, we would have paper ballots, ranked choice voting, *real* exit polls, and a president who doesn't look and act like an overcooked ham and cheese sandwich.

It's time to demand *real* elections.

NOTES

1   Frank Bajak, "Microsoft Offers Software Tools to Secure Elections," Associated Press, May 6, 2019, accessed September 26, 2019, https://www.apnews.com/7e78189c21ce4a7cb7cb73432705c3ca.

2   Devin Coldewey, "Microsoft Aims to Modernize and Secure Voting with ElectionGuard," Tech Crunch, May 6, 2019, accessed September 26, 2019, https://techcrunch.com/2019/05/06/microsoft-aims-to-modernize-and-secure-voting-with-electionguard/.

3   Whitney Webb, "Microsoft's ElectionGuard a Trojan Horse for a Military-Industrial Takeover of US Elections," MintPress News, May 24, 2019, accessed September 26, 2019, https://www.mintpressnews.com/microsoft-electionguard-a-trojan-horse-for-a-military-industrial-takeover-of-us-elections/258732/.

4   Ibid.

5   Ibid.

6   "Vault 7: CIA Hacking Tools Revealed," WikiLeaks, March 7, 2017, accessed September 26, 2019, https://wikileaks.org/ciav7p1/.

7   Webb, "Microsoft's ElectionGuard a Trojan Horse."

8   Defense Advanced Research Projects Agency, accessed September 26, 2019, https://www.darpa.mil/.

9   Webb, "Microsoft's ElectionGuard a Trojan Horse."

10   Ibid.

11   See "The Pentagon Can't Account for 21 Trillion Dollars (That's Not a Typo)," in this volume.

A FOREIGN INTERNET COMPANY RIGGED OUR ELECTIONS (AND IT WASN'T RUSSIA)

Dear reader, the following column came out several months before Cambridge Analytica became a national news story, ultimately resulting in their shameful end. This means I am either ahead of my time or sent from the future to inform past generations. I'll let you decide.

I'll be honest. I was very skeptical that a foreign internet firm could impact the votes of Americans by way of social media platforms. Considering everything that went on in the 2016 election, it kind of sounded like a gnat causing someone to lose a NASCAR race by splatting across the car's windshield. I guess, technically, you could say the car *did* lose and the gnat *did* push against its forward progress, but anyone pointing to the gnat would be an unadulterated idiot.

But I have to admit now that I was wrong. A social media data mining company has openly had an impact on our elections, and they even colluded with the Trump campaign. . . . But it's not the one you think. (And this one has probably never celebrated each moment Dolph Lundgren punched Sylvester Stallone in the face in *Rocky IV*.)

A *Forbes* article about this company says the firm has a perfect track record helping American candidates win (read: manipulating US elections).[1] And a *Guardian* article says, "The data analysis company uses a massive database of consumer and demographic information to profile and target voters" (read: this company abuses your social media information that you never wanted them to have to influence your voting patterns for or against candidates you might hate).[2]

And the company worked hand-in-tiny-hand with the Trump campaign to take aim at certain American voters in swing states. Here's just one example of how it works: the *New York Times* stated over a year ago, "[The firm] targeted Miami's Little Haiti neighborhood with messages about the Clinton Foundation's troubles in Haiti after the 2010 earthquake."[3] Even though I'm not one to have any problem with someone pointing out how incredibly flawed Hillary Clinton is/was, I do think we should know and understand the dark influences on our elections. (And that's why I've spoken so often about how our electoral system is more broken than a Jenga tower on the back seat of a public school bus in rural Alabama.)[4]

The point is—this foreign company has worked exceedingly hard specifically to manipulate American elections, and they've bragged about it in ways that are not just vague mentions of the possible influence of a troll farm that largely didn't speak English. This is real. And I, for one, am sick and tired of these *fucking Russians* meddling in. . . Oh. . . . Hold on. . . . I misread part of the article I'm sourcing. Let me rephrase that last piece: I, for one, am sick and tired of these *fucking British* meddling in our elections!

Yep. The company is Cambridge Analytica. As noted on its Wikipedia page, "Cambridge Analytica (CA) is a privately held company that combines data mining and data analysis with strategic communication for the electoral process. It was created in 2013 as an offshoot of its British parent company SCL Group to participate in American politics." As the *Washington Post* reported in 2015, "Cambridge Analytica entered the US market in 2012, according to its British chief executive Alexander Nix, and was involved in 44 US races last year."[5] (And even though the *Washington Post* has been proven to put out fake news about "Russiagate,"[6] the facts about Cambridge Analytica can be verified by more legit outlets.)

Back to the point: 44 *elections*?! . . . So there you have
it. The British meddled in our elections, colluded with the
orange dictator's campaign, and even bragged that they have
a near 100 percent success rate! I look forward to the impending indictments of these British nationals. I can't wait to see
their perp walk with the crumbs of their spotted dick still
stuck to their villainous rosy cheeks. I hope they're treated
okay in prison though. I guess it depends on whether it will
be a British prison or an American one. Recently a British
judge ruled that our prisons are tantamount to torture.[7]

Well, let's back up. Maybe we should consider Cambridge
Analytica an American company, because it is now partially
owned by hedge fund billionaire Robert Mercer,[8] who
is one of Trump's biggest campaign donors (and was
voted "Most Likely to Fund the Presidential Campaign of a
Megalomaniacal Freakshow" in high school). But Cambridge
Analytica was also very important in slanting the Brexit vote.[9]
So that means either it's a British company helping to rig
the US presidential election and 44 other elections, or it's
an American company helping to rig British votes. You get
to take your pick in this game of Foreign Meddling Bingo!

Either way, even past employees admit this company
is involved in psychological warfare. Here's an ex-employee,
quoted in the *Guardian*, talking about the time before Robert
Mercer bought into the company:

> That was before we became this dark, dystopian data
> company that gave the world Trump . . . back when we
> were still just a psychological warfare firm. . . . Psyops.
> Psychological operations—the same methods the mil-
> itary use to effect mass sentiment change. It's what
> they mean by winning "hearts and minds." We were
> just doing it to win elections in the kind of developing
> countries that don't have many rules.[10]

He's saying they were only involved in rigging the votes
of *unimportant* countries—presumably *important* countries are

those that are made up of people who a) are predominantly white and b) suffer from spasms and cold sweats when their phone battery dies.

Anyway, my point is not actually that Brits should be arrested. My point is that the recent Mueller indictments are utterly ridiculous, even if we accept that a Russian troll farm owned by a hotdog vender actively tried to influence our election (which is a big "if"). I have gone through the indictments in detail elsewhere, so I won't do that here.[11] But to heavily simplify what I've said previously, Robert Mueller has indicted 13 clickbait farmers in Russia for posting puppy memes. I'm not kidding. And, apparently, they tried to create rallies—some pro-Trump, some anti-Trump, some before the election, some after—most of them not attended by anyone (but one of them had eight people and a dog). Several of the people indicted, according to the *Washington Post*, didn't even work at the clickbait farm after 2014. And we're supposed to believe these are the supervillains rigging our election? This *has* to be a prank. I swear at some point Ashton Kutcher will jump out from behind Mueller and go, "*Aaaaa*!! *gotcha*!!"

By the way, this whole scenario is so insulting to Russia. The mighty Russian nation's *best* attempt at influencing our election consists of a baker's dozen of interns posting puppy photos from an office in St. Petersburg?! Jesus. Putin must be furious. That's honestly the *damnedest* they can do at tricking millions of Americans into voting for Trump? In that case— Russia, may I advise you to stick to Sputnik missions, because you, comrades, *suck* at rigging elections!

Meanwhile the US efforts at manipulating elections consists of bombs and war crimes and fake identities and CIA-backed warlords pretending they're populist candidates.[12] Half the guys ruling other countries right now went to Yale or some shit and roomed with a young George W. Bush (back when he was mere bad cheerleader instead of a mere bad president). Our military has poison darts if the wrong guy is about to win in another country, while the Russians apparently have a frowny emoji on Facebook? We've got planes rigged to fall out of the sky with Central American candidates in them, while Russia is apparently armed with naughty MySpace images?

They're way outmatched. Our guy wins every time. We even rigged the Russian election and bragged about it on the cover of *Time* magazine with the title—"The Secret Story of How American Advisers Helped Yeltsin Win."[13]

Yet Russia's supposed attempt at rigging our shit was literally a rally that included eight bumble-fuck Floridians with Trump posters and a dog. (And if you've seen the photo, the dog—let's be honest—probably doesn't even support Trump. He looks like more of a Jill Stein voter.) The Mueller indictments are a joke on every level. I despise Alex Jones, but he farted more Trump support after his evening pot pie than this Russian clickbait farm put out on their *best* day. Sean Hannity's acid reflux garnered more votes than these social media posts, 56 percent of which were *after* the election![14] And of the ones that appeared before the election, 25 percent were never seen by *anyone*. All of these ads only cost 6,700 dollars,[15] which in terms of campaign ad dollars is—again—a gnat on a race car. . . . Well, a gnat might be a bit big. It's closer to a *bacterium* on the gnat on the race car. This explains why Facebook's VP of ads clearly stated that influencing the election was not the goal of these Russian Facebook ads.[16]

That being said, at least these indictments are being put forward by someone with a rock-solid record of truthfulness and honor, someone who has *never* lied to the American people. . . . Oh . . . wait. . . . I'm sorry. I was thinking of someone else. In fact, Robert Mueller was head of the FBI when he said in front of Congress that there was proof of weapons of mass destruction in Iraq.[17] He was one of the most important voices to support the claim that we now know was a pile of utter horseshit so large it's still visible from space to this day. In my opinion, *no one* who put forward the WMD charade should ever be allowed in government or on television *again*. (Apparently my wishes don't pull a lot of weight, seeing as Americans are still listening to everyone from Bill Kristol to Dick Cheney to [insert name of mainstream media host here].)

But that's Mueller's résumé—lying about other countries to get us into war. That's his talent. Some people are good at card tricks or juggling or putting together intricate yet delicate mosaics. But Robert Mueller's talent lies in the ancient art of manipulating the US into war. He's not the first to do it, and he won't be the last, but he has given it his own style and panache.

Let me be clear—I understand the desire to impeach Trump. I'm in full support of impeaching Donald Trump, even though I'm not sure Mike Pence would be any better. But if we're going to impeach Trump, let's do it for something *real*! Do it for Trump's racism or his corporate corruption or his enriching himself endlessly with the presidency. Do it for his treatment of women or his idiocy or his lies. Do it for his continuous bombing of innocent men, women, and children around the world. There are *so many* good reasons to impeach that egomaniacal clown-faced man-child! But none of those reasons benefit our military-industrial complex. None of those enrich the war profiteers effectively, and therefore they are nonstarters.

Former director of the CIA James Woolsey added something very interesting to the foreign meddling debate. He was asked on Fox News whether the US has ever meddled in the elections of other countries, and he said, "Oh, probably. Back in the 1940s."[18]

Probably?! That's like asking the Secretary of Defense, "Have we ever bombed another country?" and him going, "It's likely. Ummmmm, let me check my papers here. . ."

I also enjoy Woolsey's attempted pivot to the 1940s. That's like asking a pride of lions if they've ever harmed other animals, and them responding, "Oh, probably. Back in the

1940s, I think we ate a baby giraffe, maybe? It's too far back to remember for sure. Please stop asking these questions."

Then, when the anchor pressed Woolsey on whether we continue to meddle in the elections of other countries, he laughed nervously, made a bizarre "num num num" noise (which may be some sort of software malfunction) and then responded, "But it's only for a very good cause."

Of course we're meddling in elections! According to a study out of Carnegie Mellon University, "The U.S. has a long history of attempting to influence presidential elections in other countries—it's done so as many as 81 times between 1946 and 2000."[19] And, "That number doesn't include military coups and regime change efforts following the election of candidates the U.S. didn't like, notably those in Iran, Guatemala and Chile." But have no fear, we were only doing it for a very good cause. You know us—"Every bomb we drop, every bullet we shoot, we'll be helping you." I believe that was a song by Sting. We should replace the Star-Spangled Banner with it.

I seem to recall some election meddling that didn't really help people too much. Assassinations all over the map. Backing military coups. Helping create genocides in places like Indonesia. In fact, there is growing evidence we may be preparing for military action against Venezuela as their election nears.[20] In light of our endless need to meddle in the democratic elections of every country, when political philosophy heavyweight Noam Chomsky was asked about this topic, he said, "most of the world is just collapsing in laughter" on claims that Russia intervened in the US election.[21] Well, I'm glad we could provide some entertainment for the rest of the world.

Look, even though I have a comedy show at RT America, I don't know Russia. I'm an American in America who covers American news and has never been told what to say or not to say. No one has ever censored my material, and I certainly did not support Trump (or Clinton) during the election. I don't know what the Russian government wants or doesn't want. . . . But I can read. And I know that Mueller, in his attempt to act like he's got something, has indicted a fucking clickbait farm. Now Russia's left looking like they have *no idea* how to effectively rig an election. I feel bad for them. If we believe Mueller's claim, Russia was trying to look tough and they ended up looking like they have 1/100th the power of a single Anonymous hacker. Meanwhile, we Americans act like we're facing Dr. Strangelove with his finger on the button. This is all a McCarthyist wet dream, a red scare, red herring bucket of shit.

I was a young man when America invaded Iraq, and I fell for the WMD lie, as did most of America. I watched comedian Janeane Garofalo get trashed and publicly flogged every day for having the nerve to be one of the few on television speaking out against the insanity.[22] If we had listened to her, a million Iraqis and thousands of US troops would be alive right now. I'm not fucking falling for it again. I'm not going to be a useful idiot for the war profiteers.

NOTES

1 John Koetsier, "This Big Data Marketing Firm Claims to Have a Perfect Track Record in Winning Elections," *Forbes*, November 9, 2017, accessed September 26, 2019, https://www.forbes.com/sites/johnkoetsier/2017/11/09/trumps-election-data-firm-has-100-track-record-in-winning-elections/#5f8f0c865c91.

2 Stephanie Kirchgaessner, "Cambridge Analytica Used Data from Facebook and Politico to Help Trump," *Guardian*, October 26, 2017, accessed September 26, 2019, https://www.theguardian.com/technology/2017/oct/26/cambridge-analytica-used-data-from-facebook-and-politico-to-help-trump.

3 McKenzie Funk, "Cambridge Analytica and the Secret Agenda of a Facebook Quiz," *New York Times*, November 19, 2016, accessed September 26, 2019, https://www.nytimes.com/2016/11/20/opinion/the-secret-agenda-of-a-facebook-quiz.html.

4 Redacted Tonight, "Election Fraud Special Report!" YouTube, April 29, 2016, accessed September 26, 2019, https://www.youtube.com/watch?v=TmYYvZASoks.

5 Frances Stead Sellers, "Cruz Campaign Paid $750,000 to 'Psychographic Profiling' Company," *Washington Post*, October 19, 2015,

accessed September 26, 2019, https://www.washingtonpost.com/ politics/cruz-campaign-paid-750000-to-psychographic-profiling- company/2015/10/19/6c83e508-743f-11e5-9cbb-790369643cf9_story. html?utm_term=.774f887e111a.

6   Ben Norton and Glenn Greenwald, "Washington Post Disgracefully Promotes a McCarthyite Blacklist from a New, Hidden, and Very Shady Group," Intercept, November 26, 2016, accessed September 26, 2019, https://theintercept.com/2016/11/26/washington-post- disgracefully-promotes-a-mccarthyite-blacklist-from-a-new-hidden- and-very-shady-group/.

7   Glenn Greenwald, "Citing US Prison Conditions, British Appeals Court Refuses to Extradite Accused Hacker Lauri Love to the US," Intercept, February 6, 2018, accessed September 26, 2019, https:// theintercept.com/2018/02/06/citing-u-s-prison-conditions-british- appeals-court-refuses-to-extradite-accused-hacker-lauri-love-to-the- u-s/.

8   Real News Network, "The Bizarre Far-Right Billionaire Behind Trump's Presidency," YouTube, January 13, 2017, accessed September 26, 2019, https://www.youtube.com/watch?v=uQUkaEVe7II.

9   Carole Cadwalladr, "The Great British Brexit Robbery: How Our Democracy Was Hijacked," Guardian, May 7, 2017, accessed September 26, 2019, https://www.theguardian.com/technology/2017/may/07/ the-great-british-brexit-robbery-hijacked-democracy.

10 Ibid.

11 Lee Camp, "Mueller Indictments Are A F**king Joke & It's Dangerous," YouTube, February 19, 2018, accessed September 26, 2019, https:// www.youtube.com/watch?v=n8ccn20E3v4.

12 J. Dana Stuster, "Mapped: The 7 Governments the US Has Overthrown," Foreign Policy, August 20, 2013, accessed September 26, 2019, https://foreignpolicy.com/2013/08/20/mapped-the-7-governments- the-u-s-has-overthrown/.

13 Time 148, no. 4, July 15, 1996, accessed September 26, 2019, http:// content.time.com/time/magazine/0,9263,7601960715,00.html.

14 Rob Goldman (@robjective), Twitter, February 16, 2018, accessed September 26, 2019, https://twitter.com/robjective/ status/964680123885613056?ref_src=twsrc%5Etfw&ref_url=https %3A%2F%2Fwww.zerohedge.com%2Fnews%2F2018-02- 17%2Ffacebook-vp-majority-russian-ad-spend-happened-after- election.

15 Elliot Schrage, "Hard Questions: Russian Ads Delivery to Congress," Facebook Newsroom, October 2, 2017, accessed September 26,

2019, https://newsroom.fb.com/news/2017/10/hard-questions-russian-ads-delivered-to-congress/.

16 Rob Goldman (@robjective), Twitter, February 16, 2018.

17 DZ, "Mueller Is Complicit in Run Up to Iraqi War; Weapons of Mass Destruction," YouTube, August 16, 2017, accessed September 26, 2019, https://www.youtube.com/watch?v=nkF6WpWAxy8.

18 Jon Schwarz (@schwarz), Twitter, February 17, 2018, accessed September 28, 2019, https://twitter.com/schwarz/status/964985192896221189.

19 Nina Agrawal, "The U.S. Is No Stranger to Interfering in the Elections of Other Countries," *Los Angeles Times*, December 21, 2016, accessed September 28, 2019, http://www.latimes.com/nation/la-na-us-intervention-foreign-elections-20161213-story.html.

20 Kevin Zeese and Margaret Flowers, "War Preparations against Venezuela as Election Nears," PopularResistance.org, February 18, 2018, accessed September 26, 2019, https://popularresistance.org/war-preparations-against-venezuela-as-election-nears/.

21 David N. Gibbs, "'Most of the World Is Just Collapsing in Laughter' on Claims That Russia Intervened in the US Election: An Interview with Noam Chomsky," CounterPunch, March 3, 2017, accessed September 26, 2019, https://www.counterpunch.org/2017/03/03/most-of-the-world-is-just-collapsing-in-laughter-on-claims-that-russia-intervened-in-the-us-election.

22 Fiveminutebreak, "Janeane Garofalo Pwns Fox News Channel's Brian Kilmeade," YouTube, January 8, 2007, accessed September 26, 2019, https://www.youtube.com/watch?v=3JCakTroF88.

A *NEW YORK TIMES* STORY JUST ACCIDENTALLY SHREDDED THE RUSSIAGATE HYSTERIA

Dear reader, this column came out months before the Mueller Report landed with an empty and echoing flop and Robert Mueller's testimony to Congress only made it worse. For all of Trump's crimes and corruption, it is now clear that the Russiagate conspiracy theory was a joke. So this column proved prescient.

Every once in a while, one of those stories comes along that makes the mainstream corporate media look like a bunch of middle-school kids filming their "news show" on an iPhone with their neckties crooked. Recently, one of those stories splashed down into the middle of our cultural zeitgeist like a small meteor landing in the middle of an elite dinner party. It made our mass media pundits look like hardened fools. But they have kept spouting their nonsense anyway, hoping no one notices the soup dripping down their faces. But to talk about that, I have to talk about this: last month we finally got to see the Senate report spelling out the Russian meddling in our last election. And it was a bombshell. It rocked the heart of our country. It shredded the inflamed mucousy core of our palpitating democracy.

As Dan Cohen reported for the Grayzone Project, the report said that "everything from the Green Party's Jill Stein to Instagram to Pokemon Go to the African American population had been used and confused by the deceptive Facebook pages of a private Russian troll farm called the Internet Research Agency."[1]

That's right. Russia even used Pokémon Go to pulverize the previously pristine 2016 election.[2] That's ever so frightening, since Pokémon Go is CIA-linked.[3] (I guess it's high time we just accept that the CIA has been taken over by those ruthless vodka drinkers.)

Back to the point—we learned from the report last month that the Russian Internet Research Agency manipulated every one of us with Facebook ads. If you don't mind though, the Senate and the corporate media (and anybody else who knows the secret oligarchy handshake) would really prefer you just ignore the fact that Facebook clearly stated: "56% [of the Russian ads] were after the election" and "roughly 25% of the ads were never shown to anyone."[4]

But like an overweight man dressed like Wolverine at a Comic-Con, our brave congressmen and women are not about to be dissuaded by reality. After the reports came out, Sen. Mark Warner tweeted, "Incredible. These bombshell reports demonstrate just how far Russia went to exploit the fault lines of our society and divide Americans, in an attempt to undermine and manipulate our democracy."[5]

Just after posting that, Warner patriotically pissed his red, white, and blue underoos.

So who are these amazing nonpartisan unbiased sleuths who put together this legitimate and nonpartisan unbiased Senate report? The *New York Times* found out they are a group called New Knowledge (which sounds like a terrible boy band). New Knowledge was founded by two veterans of the Obama administration, Jonathon Morgan and Ryan Fox.[6] . . . So I guess we're, um, doing away with the "nonpartisan unbiased" thing.

Well, in that case—I say go hard or go home. I want *more* bias!

The Grayzone Project pointed out that besides working for Obama and the State Department, "Morgan also developed technology for the Defense Advanced Research Projects Agency (DARPA), the arm of the Department of Defense created for basic, applied technological research, and futuristic war toys."[7]

All right, all right, not bad. But I know what you're thinking. "Lee, that might be a great bias appetizer, but we want the full bias entree!"

Okay, how about this?

"Ryan Fox is a 15-year veteran of the NSA and was a computer analyst for the Joint Special Operations Command (JSOC) military unit. JSOC is notorious for its spree of atrocities across the Middle East."[8]

Hell, yeah! You can feel that bias in your toes, can't ya? But, the truth is, we're still only at a 45 percent bias rating. I say we get it up to at least 65 percent. Back to Dan Cohen: "The report . . . was overseen by Renee DiResta, a former Wall Street trader and tech specialist who was recruited by Obama's State Department to devise strategies for combating online ISIS propaganda."[9]

So now we've got former Wall Street, former State Department, former Obama White House, former NSA, former DARPA, and former JSOC writing this completely legitimate completely factual report for the Senate about the powerful Russian impact of Facebook ads that no one ever saw.

I love it. This is like a report written by a hungry virus telling you not to wash your hands.

But hold on, it's not only this Senate report that showed nefarious Russian meddling. It's also all of those evil Russian bots. How do we know there are evil Russian bots? Well, most outlets quote Hamilton 68, which tracked Russian influence operations on Twitter.[10]

Outlets like MSNBC, the *Washington Post*, the *New York Times*, *Mother Jones*, and *Tiger Beat* are all quoting Hamilton 68 or people who are referencing work done by Hamilton 68. Well, who the hell made Hamilton 68, and why does it sound like a nineties alt-rock band that opened for Blink-182?

Oh, what do you know?! Our old friend "[Jonathon] Morgan is also one the developers of Hamilton 68. . . . Funded by the German Marshall Fund's Alliance for Securing Democracy—which is itself backed by NATO and USAID."[11]

Well, okay, that sounds pretty serious. Clearly these people have found a special device that locates Russian bots on the interwebs, and it most likely resembles the thing Egon used in the "Ghostbusters" movies. So shouldn't we just congratulate Morgan on helping to develop the holy grail for spotting Russian bots and then call it a day? Well, there's one itsy bitsy problem: one of Hamilton 68's founders, Clint Watts, admitted that the Twitter accounts it follows *may actually be real people who are not Russian at all.*[12]

Real people? Who aren't Russian? Call me crazy, but what I personally look for in a Russian bot is something that is at least Russian. And, if not that, then a bot. And, if neither, then you don't have much of a goddamn Russian bot, do ya? Claiming these are Russian bots is like saying, "I just met the Queen of England, except she may have been a small Icelandic goat."

Then, a few weeks ago, the *New York Times* revealed that New Knowledge carried out an elaborate false flag operation to hurt the election chances of Judge Roy Moore in Alabama.[13] You might recall that Roy Moore is an accused pedophile and a proven dipshit. And I don't believe he should be elected to pick the bedbugs out of Rush Limbaugh's armpits. But that doesn't mean I think these New Knowledge charlatans shouldn't be revealed for what they are.

So here's how New Knowledge's game worked, according to the *Times*. New Knowledge created a fake Facebook page to get conservatives in Alabama to support patio supply salesman Mac Watson instead of Roy Moore. New Knowledge then tried to make everyone think that Moore's campaign was working with the Kremlin by showing that he had thousands of Russian bots following his Twitter account. Many in the mainstream media ran with this outlandish idea. *Mother Jones*'s well-researched (sarcasm) article on the topic was titled "Russian Propagandists Are Pushing for Roy Moore to Win!"[14] In the article, they sourced (Can you guess?) Hamilton 68.

So to rehash: Hamilton 68, using their "Ghostbusters" device (patent pending), found that Russian bots (which may not be Russian and may not be bots and may not be Russian bots) were simply in love with alleged pedophiliac Alabama judges. So much so that a majority of their tweets (meaning at least 51 percent) were in support of Roy Moore.

But as the *New York Times* has revealed, New Knowledge's own internal report said, "We orchestrated an elaborate 'false flag' operation that planted the idea that the Moore campaign was amplified on social media by a Russian botnet."[15]

After these revelations came out a few weeks ago, Facebook suspended some of the accounts. So now the *New York Times* found itself in a quandary. They must have been thinking, "We need to report on this huge development in which the core authors of the Senate report on Russian meddling and the cofounder of Hamilton 68 were involved in lying, bullshitting, and false flagging in order to help the Democratic Party. But that *completely* undermines the Russiagate hysteria we have anchored our ship to. What do we do?"

Well, kids, take notes. This is how you do it. This is how you have your yellowcake uranium story and eat it too.

The *New York Times* headline was "Facebook Closes 5 Accounts Tied to Russia-Like Tactics in Alabama Senate Race."[16]

Russia-like tactics?! This is literally an article about how Russia was *not* involved in the Alabama senate race false flag. In fact, it's an article on how the guy who helped write the Senate report on the so-called Russian tactics is also one of the top people at New Knowledge, which either created or pushed pretend Russian bots to support Roy Moore so that they could leak to the press, "Russian bots are supporting Roy Moore!"

Sometimes the ability of the legacy media to believe (or at least regurgitate) their own bullshit is truly breathtaking.

To sum up this fuck de cluster:

- The Senate report is laughable.
- Any journalist who quotes Hamilton 68 should have their face sewn to the carpet.
- If you want ridiculous pathetic reporting on nonsense that seduces us all to the edge of nuclear annihilation, turn to your mainstream corporate media.
- If you want someone to actually put together the truth about these issues, you'll have to turn to alternative outlets.
- Bill Murray and the Ghostbusters were ahead of their time.

NOTES

1   Dan Cohen, "Senate Report on Russian Interference Was Written by Disinformation Warriors Behind Alabama 'False Flag Operation,'" Gray Zone, December 25, 2018, accessed September 26, 2019, https://grayzoneproject.com/2018/12/25/senate-report-on-russian-interference-was-written-by-disinformation-warriors-behind-alabama-false-flag-operation/.

2   Glenn Fleishman, "Russia Even Used Pokémon Go to Hack the 2016 Election. Here's How," Fortune, December 17, 2018, accessed September 26, 2019, http://fortune.com/2018/12/17/pokemon-go-russia-2016-presidential-election-hacking/.

3   Tim Hinchliffe, "CIA-backed, NSA-Approved Pokemon GO Users Give Away All Privacy Rights," Sociable, July 18, 2016, accessed September 26, 2019, https://sociable.co/technology/cia-backed-pokemon-go-privacy/.

4   Elliot Schrage, "Hard Questions: Russian Ads Delivery to Congress," Facebook Newsroom, October 2, 2017, accessed September 26, 2019, https://newsroom.fb.com/news/2017/10/hard-questions-russian-ads-delivered-to-congress/.

5   Cohen, "Senate Report on Russian Interference."

6   Scott Shane and Alan Blinder, "Secret Experiment in Alabama Senate Race Imitated Russian Tactics," New York Times, December 19, 2018, accessed September 26, 2019, https://www.nytimes.com/2018/12/19/us/alabama-senate-roy-jones-russia.html.

7   Cohen, "Senate Report on Russian Interference."

8   Ibid.

9   Ibid.

10 Elizabeth Dwoskin and Craig Timberg, "Lawmakers Press Social Media Companies—Again—on the Forces behind the #ReleaseTheMemo Campaign," *Washington Post*, January 31, 2018, accessed September 26, 2019, https://www.washingtonpost.com/news/the-switch/wp/2018/01/31/lawmakers-press-social-media-companies-again-on-the-forces-behind-the-releasethememo-campaign.

11 Cohen, "Senate Report on Russian Interference."

12 Ibid.

13 Shane and Blinder, "Secret Experiment in Alabama Senate Race."

14 Denise Clifton, "Russian Propagandists Are Pushing for Roy Moore to Win," *Mother Jones*, December 11, 2017, accessed September 26, 2019, https://www.motherjones.com/politics/2017/12/russian-propagandists-are-pushing-for-roy-moore-to-win/.

15 Shane and Blinder, "Secret Experiment in Alabama Senate Race."

16 Scott Shane, "Facebook Closes 5 Accounts Tied to Russia-Like Tactics in Alabama Senate Race," *New York Times*, December 22, 2018, accessed September 26, 2019, https://www.nytimes.com/2018/12/22/us/politics/facebook-suspends-alabama-elections.html.

WHILE OUR POLICE KILL THOUSANDS, CONGRESS WORKS TO PROTECT THE POLICE

As you read this, an American police officer will kill someone.

Or at least—statistically speaking—it's likely that in the next few hours an American police officer will extinguish the life of a fellow American. And it's an almost certainty that that person will not need to die.

How do I know this? Because our police kill roughly three people per day. American police murder more citizens in an average two-week period than cops in the United Kingdom killed in the entire twentieth century.[1] (But in their defense, for a lot of the 1900s, British bobbies were only armed with a stick. So I imagine murdering citizens took quite a lot of time and commitment, perhaps multiple guys working in shifts. Point is, there were likely very few accidental murders at the business end of the stick.)

But now the world's police almost all have guns, and this problem has become exponentially worse in America. At the beginning of May, US police had already killed 400 people in 2018.[2] To give you something to compare that with, in the 12 months preceding April 2016, British cops killed only three people and fired their weapons only seven times.[3] Seven times in a year! (I imagine your average American cop discharges his or her weapon seven times just to open a beer can when the little metal tab breaks off. And once they get it open, they fire three more shots in the air to celebrate.)

So right now, you're thinking, "I've read 15 columns on how many police murders we have. I don't need another one." However, this column is different. This one comes on the heels of Congress actually standing up and doing something about this issue in a bipartisan move (more on that in a moment).

What makes the ongoing slaughter of American people at the hands of our police so troublesome—as if that's not enough—is how incredibly rare it is for any cop to end up in jail for one of these murders. Of all of the 1,147 police killings in 2017, officers were charged with a crime in only 13—1 percent of all killings by police.[4]

Well over half of all those killings began with police responding to suspected nonviolent offenses or scenarios in which no crime had been reported. Think about that for a moment. Half the time police officers murdered someone, they weren't handling a violent crime and often were dealing with no crime at all. Basically, they thrust themselves into somebody's life, things escalated—as they tend to do when dudes with guns show up—and it ended with a state-sanctioned murder.

In a little over half of the killings, the victim had a gun. Most who were completely unarmed were people of color. This is an important point, because proponents of police murder (I don't think they call themselves that, but I do) argue that cops kill more white people than black people and therefore these killings are not racist. (For the moment, I'll put aside how odd it is to argue, "Don't worry—we're *all* being killed for no reason. So it's fine.") Yes, it is true that cops kill a lot of white people. They kill more white people than Wendy's trademarked Baconator sandwich. However, cops kill more people of color than the population percentages would dictate, and they're more likely to kill people of color who aren't armed. So while whites do lose their lives in our current police state at a ridiculous rate, they are far more likely to be waving around a gun when it happens.

Clearly, part of the problem is that US police officers have almost no fear that murdering someone could land them in trouble. Another piece of the problem is that, on average, police recruits get eight hours of training on how to de-escalate a situation. They get 58 hours of training on how to shoot things.[5] So it appears that shooting things is roughly seven times more important than trying to avoid shooting things!

Let's be honest. Eight hours of training is nothing. I received more than eight hours of training on how to put on a condom in sixth-grade sex ed—which I guess could also be called "gun safety." Granted, this particular gun safety training was pressed upon our young minds by the gym coach who doubled as our sex ed teacher. (This, by the way, is one of the most horrific experiences any kid can go through. Inevitably, the first question from the most annoying kid in the class is, "Um, coach, how do we get a girl to want to have the sexual intercourse with us?" And the coach will respond, "Son, if I knew that I wouldn't be teaching fuckin' frisbee to groups of 'shit for brains!' I'd be a millionaire selling books on how to get laid. My dog learned how to play ball quicker than you sorry sons of bitches.")

Where was I? Ah, yes, de-escalation. If police had not shot those who weren't armed with a gun, 638 more Americans would have lived to see 2018.[6] That's a 57 percent decrease in police killings.

In any profession other than that of police officer, this would be wholly unacceptable. If roofers or baristas or hair stylists were murdering more than one thousand people a year, hundreds of them unarmed, I don't think our society would be slow to respond (and I, for one, would want to know what the hell the haircuts looked like that people were still willing to brave the procedure).

But luckily, we are an evolved country. We have elected representatives who stand up for the people and defend the voters when something like this is happening. And sure enough, the House of Representatives did indeed pass a bill a couple weeks ago concerning police.

They passed the Protect and Serve Act of 2018, with only 35 representatives voting against it.[7] This is impressively shocking considering that our current Congress usually reserves that level of bipartisanship for bills giving themselves a raise or approving war criminals for cabinet positions. But rather than helping innocent civilians, the Protect and Serve Act creates enhanced penalties for anyone who intentionally causes harm to law enforcement officers.

Does that mean up until now it was legal to harm a law enforcement officer? I had no idea.

Seriously, what problem is this solving? Were loads of people punching cops in the face and then yelling, "Ha, ha! You may not like it, but it's well within my rights to beat the shit out of a cop!" No, I don't think that was a problem at all. As the Intercept put it, "[Blue Lives Matter] bills exemplify the very worst sort of legislation: at once unnecessary and pernicious."[8]

The bill is intentionally vague on what qualifies as a law enforcement officer and what qualifies as "intentionally causing harm," opening the door for even more draconian punishment of activists and protesters who get caught up in a melee and are charged with assaulting a cop, as was Occupy Wall Street protester Cecily McMillan.[9]

But it is true that even a single officer getting killed is too many, and, therefore, thank goodness Congress finally made murdering police officers illegal. . . . Oh wait, it was already *highly illegal.* When was the last time you saw a cop killer in the courtroom with his lawyer saying, "But, your honor, it was *just* a police officer. It's not like the defendant murdered a mailman or a window washer or an adorable bunny rabbit."

As professor Alex Vitale states in his excellent book, *The End of Policing,* uniformed police officers average only one felony arrest a year, meaning that most of what police do is stand around trying to find citizens to harass for small or nothing crimes.[10] They slam heads against the pavement for such violations as having an open beverage or causing a disturbance. The vast majority of cops are not fighting comic book villain Lex Luthor. And on the rare occasion you see police dressed up in their storm trooper riot outfits, they're usually getting ready to "deal with" peaceful protesters, or maybe some Native Americans who have the gall to demand clean water, or perhaps some black people who have the nerve . . . to be black people.

So if thousands of Americans were killed by police over the past decade—about half of them not even holding a gun at the time of their murders—why did Congress just fall all over itself to make assaulting police even more illegal? As Natasha Lennard put it in the Intercept:

> In our justice system, "blue lives" are already considered to matter the most—which is why police appropriation of the call for black lives to matter is so sickening. . . . The same ideological commitment to police-as-persecuted underpins FBI efforts to frame Black Lives Matter activists as potential "black identity extremists"—a designation, conjured from thin air, that claims anti-racist activism is breeding a terroristic targeting of cops.[11]

The solution? We need to heavily decrease and demilitarize our police forces. We don't need men and women with guns—above the law—running around our streets at all times. We should largely switch to community policing, in which, unless it's a truly deadly situation, you don't call the cops. You don't invite armed maniacs with a single lazy afternoon of de-escalation training into your neighborhood. Don't call the cops because your neighbor's music is too loud or some kids are fighting or you smell marijuana or a pig won't stop following you home.

Yes, last week, an Ohio man called the police on a pig that was following him home. He apparently thought, "The only people who can handle this situation are dudes with guns."[12]

How much do you want to bet that the guy who called those cops is white? Only a white guy figures the cops will help him in such a situation. If a black man called the cops to deal with a wayward pig, they'd probably shoot him. And then the following day, the cover of the local newspaper would read, "Violent African-American Shot by Police While Trying to Steal Award-Winning Pig."

NOTES

1   Matt Agorist, "American Cops Just Killed More People in March than the UK Did in the Entire 20th Century," Free Thought Project, April 6, 2015, accessed September 26, 2019, https://thefreethoughtproject.com/american-cops-killed-people-month-march-uk-entire-20th-century/.

2   "Fatal Force: 992 People Have Been Shot and Killed by Police in 2018" (graphic), *Washington Post*, last updated March 31, 2019, accessed September 26, 2019, https://www.washingtonpost.com/graphics/2018/national/police-shootings-2018/?utm_term=.5cd9713f8da9.

3   Emma Lake, "Police Shootings in the UK: How Many Have There Been in 2017 and How Many Were Fatal?" *Sun*, July 27, 2017, accessed September 26, 2019, https://www.thesun.co.uk/news/4103923/police-shootings-uk-2017/.

4   Mapping Police Violence, "2017 Police Violence Report," accessed September 26, 2019, https://policeviolencereport.org/.

5   Ibid.

6   Ibid.

7   Natasha Lennard, "Call Congress's 'Blue Lives Matter' Bills What They Are: Another Attack on Black Lives," Intercept, May 19, 2018, accessed September 26, 2019, https://theintercept.com/2018/05/19/blue-lives-matter-bill-police-brutality/.

8   Ibid.

9   Jon Swaine, "Occupy Wall Street Activist Found Guilty of Assaulting Police Officer," *Guardian*, May 5, 2014, accessed September 26, 2019, https://www.theguardian.com/world/2014/may/05/occupy-wall-street-cecily-mcmillan-guilty-assaulting-police-officer.

10   Alex S. Vitale, *The End of Policing* (London: Verso, 2017), 31.

11   Lennard, "Call Congress's 'Blue Lives Matter' Bills What They Are."

12   "Ohio Man Calls Police on Pig Following Him Home," CBS News, May 20, 2018, accessed September 26, 2019, https://www.cbsnews.com/news/elyria-ohio-man-calls-police-after-pig-follows-him-home-2018-05-20/?ftag=CNM-00-10aab7e&linkId=51943966.

OUR CRIMINAL JUSTICE SYSTEM SERVES TO PROTECT THE VILLAINS

Recently, a hero got sentenced to three years in jail. I'm not talking a traditional hero who gets saluted during halftime shows, because when he was 18, he went to a country he'd never heard of to shoot at people he'd never heard of (who we're not even technically at war with), and he did it all to get enough money to attend college, because college is too fucking expensive. We all know that's a *real* hero. No, I'm talking about a climate activism hero.

Michael Foster is one of five climate activists who broke through a chain-link fence and, in a grotesquely criminal act, shut off TransCanada's oil flow for a few hours.[1] For stopping the oil, he got three years in jail. However, for actually drilling that oil and destroying our environment, polluting the land and water, and risking our future—the heads of these oil companies get "sentenced" to zero years in jail. They instead get billions of dollars and private jets. But I bet the cocktail parties you have to attend if you're that rich are boring as sin, so the joke's on you, billionaire oil tycoons. You have boring dinners.

This proves our society is backward. The actions that are illegal vs. legal are inverted from what they should be in an evolved culture. A few weeks ago, nine activists with the organization No More Deaths were arrested for leaving jugs of water in the desert to help migrants dying of thirst.[2] That's illegal. They were charged, basically, with littering. But it's not illegal to buy up all our clean water, even near Flint, Michigan.[3] Soon, Nestlé is going to have it all, and we're going to have to bathe in Coca-Cola, because there will be no water left. We'll have to fill our water beds with small stones, and that's not comfortable.

What does *illegal* even mean anymore? In our land of the free, it's illegal to feed the homeless in some states. According to the National Coalition for the Homeless, between 2013 and 2015, "over 26 cities and communities passed laws restricting the distribution of food to the homeless, and the number is growing every year."[4] That's right, a 90-year-old was taken down to the station for the crime of handing out baked beans.[5] You may think this is ridiculous, but if you don't stop him now, what's next? Refried beans? Then, before you know it, you're involved in a pico de gallo situation. And pico de gallo leads to guacamole, and guac opens the gates to cheese, rice, and cilantro. You thought you were going to be the cool cop, look the other way, let a few beans slide, and before you know it, you're dealing with burritos, enchiladas, fajitas. And now the salsa is on your hands too.

Also illegal is housing the homeless.[6] Earlier this year, according to Splinter News, "police arrived at [a Chicago man's] house with a warrant and threatened to condemn his property unless he closed his 'unlawful basement sleeping area.'" Not illegal is taking blankets away from the homeless, as the Denver police were caught doing.[7] Also not illegal: destroying tiny homes built for the homeless. Cops did that too.[8] Banks foreclose on millions of homes, making millions of families homeless. That's not illegal. We throw out 40 percent of all food. That's not illegal.

And this isn't just a "What's the matter with us?" kind of situation. It's also a question of freedom. If I were truly free, wouldn't I be free to give somebody whatever I want? Shouldn't I be free to give away food, drinks, my Star Wars figurines, two broken umbrellas, three nose-hair trimmers, my virginity, and my award-winning collection of scabs from around the globe? Shouldn't I be allowed to give away anything I want?

The real reason we can't have people helping the homeless, giving out food and housing, is because it threatens to give a good example, to show another way forward. As *Act Out!* host Eleanor Goldfield wrote: "Filling the gaping chasms purposefully carved by capitalism and its keepers raises people's awareness; it forces them to reckon with the system they live in and ask whether or not it's worth protecting—or fighting against."[9]

Also illegal: having cocaine or heroin or selling marijuana in most states. Not illegal: making billions of dollars from the opioid crisis that's killing hundreds of thousands of people. According to the CDC, "On average, 130 Americans die every day from an opioid overdose."[10] You know how many died from smoking marijuana over the past year? One. A guy accidentally lit his sleeve on fire while he was trying to take a bong hit. Then, as he was trying to put it out, he knocked over a lamp that hit the dog. While driving the dog to an animal hospital, he drove into a mailbox and died. Marijuana: The Silent Killer.

Illegal: living off the grid. In most areas of our "Land of the Free," there are a myriad of regulations designed to make it nearly impossible to live off the grid. In fact, a lot of states consider living off the grid to be "camping." And in most places throughout the US, it is not legal to camp on your own land for more than two weeks.[11] That's right, on your own land. What does that even mean? What if I set up a tent in my living room? Would that be camping? What if I'm not camping, I just happen to be an alcoholic and pass out in my yard nightly? So much so that I start leaving a pillow and blanket and jammies out there. You may call it camping, but I call it "a regularly scheduled blackout."

It's illegal to camp in this country, yet it's legal for our military to camp out in Iraq, Afghanistan, Niger, Syria, Germany, Cuba, Djibouti, South Korea. We fucking love camping out all over the world. We have military bases in 70 percent of the world's countries. And those very assholes have the nerve to tell me I can't get a piece of land and live however the hell I want? If I decide I want to live on a 40-foot plot of dirt, wearing underwear on my head, sleeping in the grass, plugging my phone and George Foreman grill into a fecal-matter-powered generator, what does it matter to you?

Illegal: the crime of secretly filming a slaughterhouse. Yes, in some states people have been arrested for filming the abuse of farm animals.[12] Not illegal: abusing farm animals.

Also not illegal: filming every human being in this country at all times. Cameras are on every lamppost, stop light, and storefront. Soon, those cameras will have facial recognition software. Our government spies on us constantly at all hours on all our devices and says it's perfectly legal. But you bring home a tape of a piglet getting flat-out tortured, and that's not permissible, because it might harm the profits of the factory farm corporations.

Same goes for war crimes. You reveal war crimes, as Chelsea Manning did, and they're going to lock you up for a good long time. You *commit* war crimes, as our military does on a daily basis, you can become the secretary of defense. James Mattis bombed a wedding party, and then bragged he didn't lose any sleep over that decision.[13] If only he'd bombed a daycare center, he could be president by now. Come on, General Mattis, believe in yourself.

Illegal: laughing at Jeff Sessions during a Senate hearing,[14] because that type of free speech is "dangerous." On the other hand, it's completely legal to spout full-on propaganda daily like CNN or Fox News or MSNBC does. You can push for endless war while being funded by weapons contractors, and it ain't no thing. But you chuckle at an elfish-looking racist under oath saying how much he loves black people, and you get the cuffs slapped on.

Illegal: to stage a die-in protest to call attention to people murdered by police.[15] Legal: for police to murder people. And our police do it far more than any other country. US police kill more people in a day than Iceland police have killed in the past 70 years.[16] (Iceland police have killed one person in the past 70 years.)

I could go on with how backward our justice system is for hours, but here's one last one. I was in a plane recently flying over the middle of the US, and I saw something out my window that stretched for miles. As far as the eye could see, something had torn apart the Earth in a gruesome and systematic manner.[17] And then I figured out what I was looking at: fracking. From an aerial view, fracking looks like a virus on the planet. It's like the globe got smallpox. Our system is a plague on spaceship Earth. And if you try to stop the virus, you're arrested, maligned, and repressed.

At the end of the Bush administration, climate activist Tim DeChristopher tried to stop stuff like fracking. He went to an auction, posed as a bidder, and "bought" 22 thousand acres of land in Utah's pristine red rock country to stop oil and gas companies from getting it, even though he couldn't pay for it.[18] He succeeded at stopping them. He's a genuine hero. And for faking those energy lease bids, he spent two years in jail and was fined 10 thousand dollars. The parasitic rich are now above the law, and those trying to fix the system are sentenced to years in jail. This is the moral collapse of our culture and our criminal justice system. When sociopathic rulers are this powerful, they use the courts—traditionally used to stop pillaging—to continue their takeover of land and extraction of resources. They have captured the fail-safe mechanisms meant to defend against exactly this type of moral inversion.

Chris Hedges explained in February: "Oligarchs cynically view laws as mechanisms to legalize their fraud and plunder."[19] They also use the captured courts to arrest those who try to stop them. While in a Birmingham jail, Martin Luther King Jr. wrote: "One has not only a legal but a moral responsibility to obey just laws. Conversely, one has a moral responsibility to disobey unjust laws."[20] We should all seek to be illegal now.

So get out there and stop the pipelines, reveal the war crimes, and let the pico de gallo run free.

NOTES

1   Shut It Down—Climate Direct Action, "Climate Activist Michael Foster Sentenced to Three Years in Prison (Two Deferred) for Shutting Off Keystone Tar Sands Pipeline in North Dakota," Common Dreams, February 6, 2018, accessed September 26, 2019, https://www.commondreams.org/newswire/2018/02/06/climate-activist-michael-foster-sentenced-three-years-prison-two-deferred.

2   Jay Willis, "The Border Activist Charged for Providing Water to Migrants Could Still Face Legal Jeopardy," *GQ*, June 12, 2019, accessed September 26, 2019, https://www.gq.com/story/scott-warren-jury-deadlocks; also see No More Deaths, accessed September 26, 2019, http://forms.nomoredeaths.org/en/.

3   "Michigan's Water Wars: Nestlé Pumps Millions of Gallons for Free While Flint Pays for Poisoned Water," Democracy Now! February 17, 2016, accessed September 26, 2019, https://www.democracynow.org/2016/2/17/michigans_water_wars_nestle_pumps_millions.

4   National Coalition for the Homeless, "Illegal to Be a Good Samaritan," July 17, 2015, accessed September 26, 2019, http://nationalhomeless.org/good-samaritan/.

5   Kevin Conlon and Catherine E. Shoichet, "90-Year-Old Florida Man Charged for Feeding Homeless People," CNN, November 4, 2014, accessed September 26, 2019, https://www.cnn.com/2014/11/04/justice/florida-feeding-homeless-charges/index.html.

6   Rafi Schwartz, "Chicago Suburb Threatens Man for Daring to Offer Homeless People a Place to Sleep," Splinter, January 5, 2018, accessed September 26, 2019, https://splinternews.com/chicago-suburb-threatens-man-for-daring-to-offer-homele-1821803157.

7   Liam Quinn, "'They Don't Give a F*** if I Die Out Here in This Cold Weather': Denver Police Forced to Defend Officers After They Were Filmed Taking Blankets from Homeless People on a Freezing Night," *Daily Mail*, December 16, 2016, accessed September 26, 2019, http://www.dailymail.co.uk/news/article-4041760/Denver-police-forced-defend-officers-took-blankets-homeless-people.html.

8   Denver Homeless Out Loud, "Tiny Homes Destroyed by City 10 Arrested" (press release), October 25, 2015, accessed September

26, 2019, https://denverhomelessoutloud.org/2015/10/25/tiny homes-destroyed-by-city-10-arrested/.

9   Eleanor Goldfield, "This Is Why No Good Deed Goes Unpunished," Art Killing Apathy, February 12, 2018, accessed September 26, 2019, https://www.artkillingapathy.com/why-no-good-deed-goes-unpunished/.

10   "Understanding the Epidemic," Centers for Disease Control and Prevention, last revised December 19, 2018, accessed September 26, 2019, https://www.cdc.gov/drugoverdose/epidemic/index.html.

11   Eric, "Off Grid Living Is Illegal! Sort Of. . .," Off Grid World, accessed September 26, 2019, https://offgridworld.com/off-grid-living-is-illegal-sort-of/.

12   John Vibes, "Activists Charged Under Ag-Gag Law for Taking Pictures of a Pig Farm from Public Property," Free Thought Project, January 13, 2015, accessed September 26, 2019, http://thefreethoughtproject.com/activists-charged-filming-factory-farms-public-property-ag-gag-law/.

13   Rory McCarthy, "US Soldiers Started to Shoot Us, One by One," *Guardian*, May 20, 2004, accessed September 26, 2019, https://www.theguardian.com/world/2004/may/21/iraq.rorymccarthy.

14   Ryan J. Reilly, "Jury Convicts Woman Who Laughed at Jeff Sessions During Senate Hearing," HuffPost, May 3, 2017, accessed September 26, 2019, https://www.huffingtonpost.com/entry/jeff-sessions-laugh-congressional-hearing_us_590929bbe4b05c39768420ef.

15   Andrew Couts, "Eric Garner 'Die In' Protest Takes Over New York's Grand Central Terminal," Daily Dot, December 3, 2014, accessed September 26, 2019, https://www.dailydot.com/layer8/eric-garner-die-in-grand-central-new-york/.

16   Jamiles Lartey, "By the Numbers: US Police Kill More in Days Than Other Countries Do in Years," *Guardian*, June 9, 2015, accessed September 26, 2019, https://www.theguardian.com/us-news/2015/jun/09/the-counted-police-killings-us-vs-other-countries.

17   Lauren McCauley, "Fracking-Induced Earthquakes Highlighted in New USGS Map," Common Dreams, April 23, 2015, accessed September 26, 2019, https://www.commondreams.org/news/2015/04/23/fracking-induced-earthquakes-highlighted-new-usgs-map.

18   "Posing as a Bidder, Utah Student Disrupts Government Auction of 150,000 Acres of Wilderness for Oil & Gas Drilling," Democracy Now! December 22, 2008, accessed September 26, 2019, https://www.democracynow.org/2008/12/22/posing_as_a_bidder_utah_student.

19   Chris Hedges, "The Deadly Rule of the Oligarchs," Truthdig, February 11, 2018, accessed September 26, 2019, https://www.truthdig.com/articles/deadly-rule-oligarchs/.

20 Martin Luther King Jr., "Letter from a Birmingham Jail," University of Pennsylvania African Studies Center, April 16, 1963, accessed September 26, 2019, https://www.africa.upenn.edu/Articles_Gen/ Letter_Birmingham.html.

THREE NEW STUDIES THAT WILL MAKE YOU RETHINK SYSTEMIC RACISM

Racism is like sewage. Whether we're currently engaging in a national dialogue about it or not, it's still there. It runs under our streets, our buildings, our society. Millions of tons of shit.

A few months ago, a national dialogue about race bubbled up to the surface in all its stinking, rancid glory. That dialogue flared up when we all found out that the governor of my home state of Virginia, Ralph Northam, appeared in his medical school yearbook photo wearing blackface beside someone in a Klan hood (or perhaps it was him in the Klan hood next to a guy in blackface—neither explanation really helps his case).[1] And, in that moment, we could all see what racism looks like. It was tangible. It was real. We could point to it and cringe.

That kind of racism is actually rare. More often, it trickles along beneath our collective consciousness, quietly infecting everything.

Systemic racism is not as obvious, and a lot of people try to claim it no longer exists. "It's gone. What systemic racism? *Black Panther* was one of the most popular movies *ever*, therefore, racism is over," they claim.

Unfortunately, it doesn't work like that.

Three recent studies prove just how many millions of gallons of fetid, systemic racism still fill our country. Let's start with education. A couple months ago, a new report found a 23-billion-dollar racial funding gap for schools. The report stated: "Overwhelmingly white school districts received $23 billion more than predominantly non-white school districts in state and local funding in 2016, despite serving roughly the same number of children."[2]

Let me repeat that number so it echoes in your head: 23 *billion dollars!* The following should go without saying, but I'm going to say it anyway, because I'm kind of a dick that way: education is important.

A kid's entire life can rest on the type of early schooling he or she receives. A good education creates opportunities; a bad education shuts doors in a child's future face. (I don't mean she has a face from the future or even a futuristic face. I mean in the future, the door is shut in her face. You probably knew that.)

In schools with the most funding, students are given laptop computers and trained to succeed. In the least funded schools, teachers dole out antiquated textbooks that say dinosaurs were large frogs and slavery was just an early American internship program that got out of hand.

This is when the squishy liberals say, "Lee, that's because we have a racist president who hates funding the education of people of color." And while I agree that having a racist president doesn't help matters, that 23 billion dollars is from 2016, while President *Obama* was still in office.

Squishy liberals then reply, "But that can't be. I thought Obama ended all racial inequality and brought love and Tootsie Pops to the world."

No, not exactly. You're only two words off, though. Obama ended all *reporting on* racial inequality. Fewer people mentioned the sewage under our society when he held the highest office. You see the difference? The cold truth is that systemic racism against black, Hispanic, and Indigenous people exists no matter who's in the White House.

Let's move on to climate change. There can't possibly be racial disparity when it comes to weather, could there? Hurricanes don't exactly hit only black neighborhoods.

True. But racist policies often come into play after the storms or flood waters have subsided.

A new NPR investigation "found that white communities nationwide have disproportionately received more federal buyouts after a disaster than communities of color."[3]

One of FEMA's services for disaster-ravaged towns is to purchase damaged properties when people don't want to live there anymore. Yet according to the NPR report:

> Federal disaster aid is allocated based on a cost-benefit calculation meant to minimize taxpayer risk. That means money is not necessarily doled out to those who need it most but rather to those whose property is worth more—and to those who own property in the first place.[4]

This fact kind of blew me away. We have created a Federal Emergency Management Agency *designed* to help the rich the most after a horrible disaster. Just off the top of your head, who do you think needs the most help after a natural disaster? I'll give you a hint—it's the poor.

This whole thing would be sort of funny if you read it in a satirical novel about a dystopian future or something. But seeing as it's written by our government, it's about as funny as flesh-eating bacteria.

In this particular instance, systemic racism does not originate in race but in the way the rich have crafted our laws and our systems to favor the rich. So it's a class issue rather than a race issue. Unfortunately, other factors of systemic racism—such as hiring practices and who gets promoted—ensure that white people are more likely to be extremely wealthy and less likely to be extremely poor. Therefore, our country has a racial wealth gap the size of the Grand Canyon (only it's a much less fun tour).

Workplace racism would require an entirely separate column, so I won't get into it here, other than to point out you're 50 percent less likely to get the first interview for a job if you have a black-sounding name.[5]

Back to the wealth gap. According to a Duke University paper titled "What We Get Wrong About Closing the Racial Wealth Gap":

> Data from 2014 shows that black households hold less than 7 cents on the dollar compared to white households. The white household living near the poverty line typically has about $18,000, while black households in similar economic straits typically have a median wealth near zero. This means many black families have a negative net worth.[6]

That gigantic wealth gap affects where people live, and that brings us to our third study, which finds a racial gap between who creates air pollution and who is forced to inhale it.[7]

If you're like me, you're now thinking, "Oh, come on! I know white people can be dicks, but I've never seen an angry white guy with petrochemicals shooting out his ass. What are these researchers talking about?"

Well, according to the report, they're saying:

> While we tend to think of factories as the source of pollution, those polluters wouldn't exist without consumer demand for the products. . . . Air pollution is disproportionately caused by white Americans' consumption of goods and services, but disproportionately inhaled by black and Hispanic Americans.[8]

Okay, I'll begrudgingly grant them that. But has anyone stopped to ask why black and Hispanic Americans choose to breathe so much?! Slow it down. Skip every other breath (just like people do when they're around Rush Limbaugh). Have some will power!

This study shows that due to the wealth gap and population differences, white people create the majority of the pollution in our country. Minorities then end up breathing it in their air or drinking it in their water, because they more often live in corporate sacrifice zones—areas where the property value is lower and corporations feel free to destroy the landscape. And, again, that comes back to the wealth gap.

(If I'm honest, as a white person, I'm not surprised that white people create the most pollution by using and buying the most stuff. I have family members who own polish for the shoe tree that holds the shoes their pet rabbit wears. They own knitted cozies for remote controls that go to cordless devices that do things they don't need done. They buy things to take care of things that go on things that attach to nothing! And making those meaningless things creates pollution, and then a nonwhite person has to breathe in goddamn rabbit shoes. You know how many microparticles of bedazzled cell phone cases non-white people drank in their water last year?! It's a fucked-up system, to say the least.)

All told, much of our systemic racism problem comes down to class and wealth, not just race. But race, class, and wealth are deeply, inexorably linked. And therefore, whether you choose to ignore it or not, we must acknowledge that systemic racism is a thing. It's in our schools, our air, our water, and even our televisions. It impacts every area of our lives, and much like climate change, we need to start fixing it rather than acting like it doesn't exist.

NOTES

1   Mike Valerio, "Northam Blackface Yearbook Investigation Will Be Made Public: Inquiry Ongoing," WUSA9, April 1, 2019, accessed September 26, 2019, https://www.wusa9.com/article/news/northam-blackface-yearbook-investigation-will-be-made-public-inquiry-ongoing/65-e051e5d1-5e4d-4015-bb1d-c9238d8e9dac.

2   Laura Meckler, "Report Finds $23 Billion Racial Funding Gap for Schools," Washington Post, February 26, 2019, accessed September 26, 2019, https://www.washingtonpost.com/local/education/report-

finds-23-billion-racial-funding-gap-for-schools/2019/02/25/
d562b704-3915-11e9-a06c-3ec8ed509d15_story.html?noredirect=
on&utm_term=.9ac852883cd2.

3   Robert Benincasa, "Search the Thousands of Disaster Buyouts FEMA
     Didn't Want You to See," NPR, March 5, 2019, accessed September
     26, 2019, https://www.npr.org/2019/03/05/696995788/search-the-
     thousands-of-disaster-buyouts-fema-didnt-want-you-to-see.

4   Ibid.

5   Marianne Bertrand and Sendhil Mullainathan, "Are Emily and Greg
     More Employable Than Lakisha and Jamal? A Field Experiment
     on Labor Market Discrimination," National Bureau of Economic
     Research working paper 9873, July 2003, accessed September 26, 2019,
     https://www.nber.org/papers/w9873.pdf.

6   William Darity Jr., Darrick Hamilton, Mark Paul, Alan Aja, Anne
     Price, Antonio Moore, and Caterina Chiopris, *What We Get Wrong
     About Closing the Racial Wealth Gap*, Samuel DuBois Cook Center on
     Social Equity/Insight Center for Community Economic Development,
     April 2018, accessed September 26, 2019, https://socialequity.duke.
     edu/sites/socialequity.duke.edu/files/site-images/FINAL%20
     COMPLETE%20REPORT_.pdf.

7   Johnathan Lambert, "Study Finds Racial Gap between Who
     Causes Air Pollution and Who Breathes It," NPR, March 11, 2019,
     accessed September 26, 2019, https://www.npr.org/sections/health-
     shots/2019/03/11/702348935/study-finds-racial-gap-between-who-
     causes-air-pollution-and-who-breathes-it.

8   Ibid.

EIGHTEEN WAYS JULIAN ASSANGE CHANGED THE WORLD

Julian Assange is a dick. It's important you understand that.

Assange and WikiLeaks revealed the American military's war crimes, the American government's corruption, and the American corporate media's pathetic servile flattery of the power elite. So if you're a member of our ruling class, you would view those as textbook examples of dickery.

In a moment, I'm going to list all the ways Julian Assange changed the world by being a dick.

In an evolved and fully realized society, the oligarchy would see Assange as a dangerous criminal (which they do), and the average working men and women would view him as justice personified (which they don't). We would celebrate him even as the mass media told us to hope for his downfall—like a Batman or a Robin Hood or an Ozzy Osbourne (the early years, not the "cleaning dog turds off his carpet" years).

But we are not evolved, and this is not Gotham City, and average Americans don't root for the truth. Many Americans cheer for Assange's imprisonment. They believe the corporate plutocratic talking points and yearn for the days when we no longer have to hear about our country's crimes against humanity or our bankers' crimes against the economy. Subconsciously they must believe that a life in which we're tirelessly exploited by rich villains and know all about it thanks to the exhaustive efforts of an eccentric Australian is worse than one in which we're tirelessly exploited by rich villains yet know nothing about it.

"Ignorance is bliss" is the meditative mantra of the United States of America.

Julian Assange has been arrested and is now locked away in British custody. The US government wants to extradite him, regardless of the official version, for the crime of revealing our government's crimes.[1] Nearly every government on our third rock from the sun despises the man for bringing transparency to the process of ruling the unwashed masses. (The level of wash has, however, increased thanks to aggressive marketing campaigns from a variety of shampoo brands.)

It is politically inconvenient at this time for the screaming corporate news to remind our entire citizenry what exactly WikiLeaks has done for us. So you won't see the following list of WikiLeaks' accomplishments anywhere on your corporate airwaves—in the same way the mainstream media did not begin every report about Chelsea Manning's trial with a rundown of the war crimes she helped reveal.

And Chelsea Manning's most famous leak is arguably also WikiLeaks' most famous leak, so it'll top this list:

1. That would be the notorious collateral murder video, showing US air crew gunning down unarmed Iraqi civilians with an enthusiasm that couldn't be matched by an eight-year-old winning a five-foot-tall stuffed animal at the county fair.[2] They murdered between 12 and 18 innocent people, two of them Reuters journalists. Zero people have been arrested for the collateral murders. Yet Julian Assange has been arrested *for revealing them.*

2. WikiLeaks brought us the Guantanamo Bay "Camp Delta Standard Operating Procedures"[3]—showing that many of the prisoners held in the US military detention facility were completely innocent, and that some were hidden from Red Cross officials.

(Because when you're torturing innocent people,
you kinda want to do that in peace and quiet, away
from prying eyes. It's very easy to get distracted,
and then you lose your place and have to start *all
over again*.) None of the soldiers torturing innocent
people at Gitmo have been arrested for it. Yet Julian
Assange has been *arrested for revealing it*.

3.   Not content with revealing only war crimes,
WikiLeaks in 2008 came out with the secret bibles
of Scientology,[4] which showed that aliens, um, run
the world or . . . aliens are inside all of us or . . .
aliens give us indigestion. I can't really remember.
But no one has ever been arrested for perpetrating
that nutbag cult. Yet Julian Assange has been *for
revealing it*.

Many people believe WikiLeaks has unveiled only crimes
of the American government, but that's completely false.
The US corporate media doesn't want average Americans to
understand that WikiLeaks has upped the level of transparency around the world.

4–9. WikiLeaks posted videos of Tibetan dissidents in
China fighting back, videos which were not allowed
to be viewed in China. They revealed the Peru oil
scandal and that Russia was spying on its citizens' cell phones and the Minton Report on toxic
dumping in Africa and the Syria Files—showing
the inner workings of the Syrian government. And
WikiLeaks displayed to the global audience a secret
Australian supreme court gag order that stopped the
Australian press from reporting on a huge bribery
scandal that involved the central bank and international leaders. Assange is hated by governments
around the world. As much as they may like transparency when it comes to other countries (specifically

the United States), they don't want *their own* particular piles of shit on full display. It's kinda like when most people laugh heartily after an up-skirt photo of a celebrity is published in the tabloids, but, at the same time, none of us want up-skirt photos *of us* all over the web. (I know I don't, because I haven't shaved up there since Carter was in office.) As far as I know, none of the political figures involved in these scandals have gone to prison for participating in them. Yet Julian Assange has *for revealing them.*

10. Let's not forget the Iraq War logs—hundreds of thousands of documents relating to America's illegal invasion of Iraq,[5] which we called a "war," but I think a war needs to have two sides. Iraq's elite Republican Guard turned out to be three guys and a donkey . . . and the donkey didn't even have good aim. So far as I can tell, no one committing the war crimes evidenced in the Iraq War logs has been locked up for them. Yet Julian Assange has been *for revealing them.*

11. WikiLeaks showed us the highly secretive Bilderberg Group meeting reports.[6] The Bilderberg Group is made up of incredibly powerful men and women who get together and decide how to rule over all of us street people, all the while sitting on thrones made from the bones of the babies of nonbelievers. They're often accused of being lizard people, but really they're just regular ol' sociopaths with lizard skin they purchased from a plastic surgeon in Malibu for half a million dollars. I don't think anyone from the Bilderberg Group is being tortured in solitary confinement right now. Yet Julian Assange is *for revealing who they are.*

12. The Barclays Bank tax avoidance scheme netted Barclays one billion pounds a year.[7] While it was

ordered to pay 500 million pounds in lost taxes, no one was arrested for that theft from citizens. Yet Julian Assange was *for revealing it*.

13. The Afghan War Diaries consisted of 92 thousand documents related to our destruction of Afghanistan. They detailed friendly fire incidents and civilian casualties. According to WikiLeaks, the diaries showed that "When reporting their own activities U.S. Units are inclined to classify civilian kills as insurgent kills, downplay the number of people killed or otherwise make excuses for themselves."[8] It's tough to read this without being floored at the comedy routine that our military actions have become. I picture this scenario happening every day in Afghanistan:

> US Soldier no. 1: This guy we just killed was an insurgent.
> US Soldier no. 2: How do you know?
> US Soldier no. 1: Because we killed him.
> US Soldier no. 2: Why'd we kill him?
> US Soldier no. 1: Because he's an insurgent.
> US Soldier no. 2: How do you know?
> US Soldier no. 1: Because we killed him.
> (Repeat until lightheaded.)

I am unaware of anyone locked away for these war crimes. Yet Julian Assange is locked away *for revealing them*.

14. WikiLeaks also unveiled hundreds of thousands of US State Department cables that showed more clearly than ever how our secretive government rules its empire with little to no input from the American people.[9] Among many other things, the cables revealed Secretary of State Hillary Clinton ordered diplomats to spy on French, British, Russian, and

Chinese delegations at the UN Security Council. It also showed that Arab nations urged the US to strike Iran, and much more. Our ruling elite, of course, view this as a massive breach of national security. That's understandable. But that worldview comes into play only if you think the elites are the only ones who should know how our nation is run. To answer this question for yourself, do the following experiment. Pull up a photo of Donald Trump—a really close-up image of his blister-colored, bulbous face. Now, look at it intensely for five minutes. . . . After you've done that, tell me you want the ruling elite to be the only ones who know what the fuck is going on. (Go ahead and try it—I'll wait.) Ostensibly, the concept of our government was that the ruling class would be accountable to us, the average Americans. To you and me. To the workers and the number crunchers. To the single moms and the cashiers and the street sweepers and the fluffers on the porn sets. We're supposed to vote based on our knowledge of how our government is functioning. But if the entirety of our representatives' criminal behavior is labeled top secret for national security purposes, then we aren't really an informed populace, *are we*? So for all that was unveiled in the State Department cables, no one has been locked up. But Julian Assange has been *for revealing them*.

15. The Stratfor emails—this was millions of emails that showed how a private intelligence agency was used by its US corporate and government clients to target activists and protesters.[10] No one at Stratfor is currently locked away. But Julian Assange is *for revealing the truth*.

16. Then there's the trade deals—TPP, TISA, and TTIP—all three amount to one of the largest

attempts at corporate takeover ever conceived. All three were more secretive than Donald Trump's taxes. Government officials and corporate lawyers and lobbyists wrote every word in private. Not even Congress saw the Trans-Pacific Partnership until very late in the process. The only organization to show the American citizens (and European citizens) some of those documents before they were made into law? WikiLeaks. WikiLeaks made us aware of the corporate restraints that were about to be placed on us, and that's what allowed activists to pressure Trump to pull out of the TPP.[11] None of those secretive corporate titans are imprisoned for their attempted power grab, but Julian Assange is *for revealing it.*

17. The DNC emails.[12] I'll explain for those of you who have been living in a cave that is itself inside a "yellow and blue makes green" sealed Tupperware container. The Democratic National Committee's emails gave us proof of just how rigged the Democratic primaries really are. They proved that the media was in bed with Hillary Clinton's campaign. They even showed that Obama's entire first-term cabinet was selected by Citibank. Yes, Citibank. (I would find it less offensive if his cabinet had been decided by a rabid raccoon or the pus oozing out of Darth Vader's face or Vince McMahon's concussed frontal lobe.) Whatever election integrity movement exists right now, it owes a lot to these revelations by WikiLeaks. After being sued over this matter, the DNC's lawyers admitted in court that the DNC has no obligation to have a fair primary election.[13] It's their right to rig it. (But don't try to get angry about this, because if you do, the CIA has myriad ways to fuck up your life.) No one is in

prison for rigging the primaries but Julian Assange is *for revealing* it.

18. In 2017, WikiLeaks posted a trove of CIA documents called "Vault 7."[14] It detailed their capabilities, including remotely taking over cars, smart TVs, web browsers, and smartphones. After I found out about that, for a solid two weeks I thought, "Screw it. I'm going full Amish. One hundred percent. Let's see the CIA hack my butter churn. Are they going to use backdoor software to get inside my rustic wooden bow saw? Even if they could, what are they going to listen to—my conversation about how mee bobblin fraa redd up for rutschin' 'round. Say no more! Schmunzla wunderbar!" So is anybody at the CIA chained up for violating our privacy in every way possible? No, but Julian Assange is *for revealing* it.

By thrusting the truth upon the people of Earth, WikiLeaks helped create movements worldwide like the Arab Spring and Occupy. And don't forget, at first WikiLeaks and Assange were celebrated for their amazing work. In 2011 even Amnesty International hailed WikiLeaks as one of the Arab Spring catalysts. The *Guardian* said:

> The year 2010 may well be remembered as a watershed year when activists and journalists used new technology to speak truth to power and, in so doing, pushed for greater respect for human rights. . . . It is also the year when repressive governments faced the real possibility that their days were numbered.[15]

So why have so many outlets and people turned against Assange and WikiLeaks? Because it turned out he wasn't revealing only repressive Arab regimes. He also revealed US-backed coups and war crimes around the world. He exposed the criminality and villainy of the American ruling elite.

Nothing published on WikiLeaks has ever been proven untrue. Compare that record to CNN, MSNBC, Fox News, or any mainstream outlet. Assange has been nominated for multiple Nobel Peace Prizes, and nearly every respected media outlet has used source material from WikiLeaks in their reporting. Yet in spite of all this and after seven years in captivity, the man who laid bare our criminal leaders and showed each one of us our chains is not receiving parades and accolades. He and those who helped him reveal the truth are the only ones endlessly punished.

We are all Julian Assange. As long as he's imprisoned, we can never be free.

NOTES

1   Natasha Lomas, "Julian Assange Jailed for 50 Weeks for Breaching UK Bail Conditions," Tech Crunch, May 1, 2019, accessed September 26, 2019, https://techcrunch.com/2019/05/01/julian-assange-jailed-for-50-weeks-for-breaching-uk-bail-conditions/.

2   "Collateral Murder," WikiLeaks, April 5, 2010, accessed September 26, 2019, https://collateralmurder.wikileaks.org/.

3   Ryan Singel, "Sensitive Guantánamo Bay Manual Leaked through Wiki Site," Wired, November 14, 2007, accessed September 26, 2019, https://www.wired.com/2007/11/gitmo-2/.

4   "Watchdog Web Site Draws Legal Threats from Scientologists, Mormons," Fox News, June 19, 2008, accessed September 26, 2019, https://www.foxnews.com/story/watchdog-web-site-draws-legal-threats-from-scientologists-mormons.

5   Nick Davies, Jonathan Steele, and David Lee, "Iraq War Logs: Secret Files Show How US Ignored Torture," Guardian, October 22, 2010, accessed September 28, 2019, https://www.theguardian.com/world/2010/oct/22/iraq-war-logs-military-leaks.

6   Aaron Kesel, "Explosive Evidence Official Bilderberg Group Documents Leaked," We Are Change, June 25, 2016, accessed September 28, 2019, https://wearechange.org/classified-bilderberg-group-documents-leaked/.

7   "Barclays 'Makes £1bn a Year' through Tax Avoidance Schemes," Daily Mail, March 15, 2009, accessed September 26, 2019, https://www.dailymail.co.uk/news/article-1162148/Barclays-makes-1bn-year-tax-avoidance-schemes.html.

8   Tim King, "Wikileaks Releases 'The Afghan War Diary,'" Salem News, July 25, 2010, accessed September 26, 2019, http://salem-news.com/articles/july252010/wikileaks-afghan.php.

9   Jonathan Karl, Bradley Blackburn, and Dean Schabner, "WikiLeaks Releases Confidential Diplomat Cables," ABC News, November 28, 2010, accessed September 26, 2019, https://abcnews.go.com/Politics/wikileaks-releases-classified-diplomat-cables-us-state-department/story?id=12260376.

10   James Ball, "WikiLeaks Releases First 200 of 5m Stratfor Emails," *Guardian*, February 27, 2012, accessed September 26, 2019, https://www.theguardian.com/media/2012/feb/27/wikileaks-stratfor-emails-anonymous.

11   Public Citizen/Third World Network, "WikiLeaks Publishes Final TPP Intellectual Property Text Analysis," WikiLeaks, October 9, 2015, accessed September 26, 2019, https://wikileaks.org/tpp-ip3/biologics/Ambiguity%20Leads%20to%20Fallacy%20(Biologics).pdf.

12   Alana Abramson and Shushannah Walshe, "The 4 Most Damaging Emails from the DNC WikiLeaks Dump," ABC News, July 25, 2016, accessed September 26, 2019, https://abcnews.go.com/Politics/damaging-emails-dnc-wikileaks-dump/story?id=40852448.

13   Alberto Luperon, "DNC Lawyer Admits They Weren't Required to Be Impartial Between Clinton, Sanders," Law and Crime, April 29, 2017, accessed September 26, 2019, https://lawandcrime.com/high-profile/dnc-lawyer-reportedly-said-they-could-have-chosen-between-clinton-sanders-over-cigars-in-back-rooms/.

14   "WikiLeaks Posts Trove of CIA Documents Detailing Mass Hacking," CBS News, March 7, 2017, accessed September 26, 2019, https://www.cbsnews.com/news/wikileaks-cia-documents-released-cyber-intelligence/.

15   Peter Walker, "Amnesty International Hails WikiLeaks and Guardian as Arab Spring 'Catalysts,'" *Guardian*, May 13, 2011, accessed September 26, 2019, https://www.theguardian.com/world/2011/may/13/amnesty-international-wikileaks-arab-spring/.

SIX WAYS THE "RESISTANCE" GAVE TRUMP A DICTATOR'S TOOLKIT

My longtime archnemesis, the Trans-Pacific Partnership (TPP)—which I thought we had vanquished after years of stabbing, kicking, and choking it—may now be rising from the dead like a zombie, like a vampire, like a Jeff Sessions. And this is yet another sign that the so-called Democratic "resistance" is a joke so big it has to buy two airplane seats.

Let me explain.

The TPP was the largest trade deal ever conceived. It was created under Barack Obama, hashed out in secrecy by corporate lawyers, involved 12 countries, and would've gone through except that Donald Trump promised during his campaign he would not sign it. When he got into office, he stuck to that promise. But don't kid yourself into thinking he trashed it, because he had some strong economic understanding of how harmful this beast would've been to the working class, or that he cared a lot for the environment and the people the TPP would have hurt.

Not at all.

He wasn't sobbing at his desk thinking about the young child getting paid pennies a day, because corporations can exploit everyone freely. Instead, Trump binned it because a bunch of people on Twitter yelled at him, and he thought: "Whatever they said—I'll do that. Plus, it will piss off Obama."

So as idiots and paint chip nibblers are known to do, Trump did something good for all the wrong reasons. That's pretty much the case every time he does something good. Anyway, now Australia is pressing Donald to rejoin the TPP. And recently Trump said he "would do TPP if we were able to make a substantially better deal."[1] There's also the risk that Trump and friends will basically just rename the TPP something else. You know, rebrand it so the American people will stop complaining. Instead of "Trans-Pacific Partnership," it will become the "Trans-Fats Are Tasty Partnership," and Americans will think: "That sounds good. You mean like Oreos and stuff? Like Double-Stuffed Oreos and stuff? Mmmmmmm, stuffffff."

Of course, this raises questions: What does "a better deal" even *mean* to Trump? You know he's not going to read the thing. It's thousands of pages long!

He's also renegotiating NAFTA to "get us a better deal," which is like hiring an empty shoe box to renegotiate your mortgage.[2] And keep in mind, NAFTA was not just a disaster for your average American. It was a disaster for your average Mexican too, which triggered much of the migration to the United States that Trump supporters and run-of-the-mill racists love to complain about. NAFTA allowed US corporations to crush Mexican farmers, and suddenly, trekking through the deadly desert to America seemed like a nice option.

What does this have to do with the so-called Democratic "resistance"? Well, there's a reason Trump has such an outsize trade authority—a reason your mainstream media would rather you forget. Obama handed this trade authority to Trump on a silver platter. Back in 2015, Congress, under pressure from the Obama administration, voted to give the president, *any* president, unlimited trade authority for the next six years.[3] This means Congress cannot change a word of any trade deal Trump approves.

This is yet another way the corporate-owned Democrats have furthered and supported Donald Trump every step of the way. They try to act like the "resistance," but they're not resisting anything. They're trying desperately to prop him up, make him stronger, give him every power a unitary executive can have.

Think about this. Besides unlimited trade authority, many Democrats also voted to continue to give Trump unlimited war powers with the Authorization for Use of Military Force (AUMF).[4] Thirteen Democratic senators voted to continue to have no congressional oversight over Trump's wars. Remember that the next time Jean Shaheen, Claire McCaskill, Mark Warner, and Sheldon Whitehouse try to tell you they're "part of the resistance." No, they're "part of the freesistance"—giving Trump a free pass for unlimited war. They're paid employees of the war profiteers. Having the word "Senator" before your name just means you're one of the more *highly paid* employees. It just means you have a bathroom that others aren't allowed to use.

A few weeks ago, Congress passed a spending bill that took away the remaining congressional oversight of the intelligence community. Before that, they voted to continue giving Trump unlimited surveillance abilities.[5] According to the Intercept:

> Leading the charge against reforms of the FBI's domestic spying powers was Rep. Adam Schiff of California, the ranking member of the House Intelligence Committee who, in countless TV appearances, has strongly insinuated, if not outright stated, that Trump is controlled by and loyal to Russian President Vladimir Putin.

Huh, that's interesting. If Schiff believes Trump is controlled by Putin, which would be treasonous, then you would think Schiff must *really not* want Trump to have a dictator's toolbox. Yet Schiff has fought for Trump to have unlimited spying abilities, unlimited war powers, and unlimited trade authority (which means unlimited rights to cede our nation's sovereignty to corporations). Wow, it almost sounds as if Schiff is just saying that stuff about Putin because it looks good to be "part of the resistance."

By the way, it's not as if Schiff sheepishly voted for these surveillance powers. The Intercept's Glenn Greenwald wrote: "In demanding rejection of the warrant requirement safeguard, Schiff channeled Dick Cheney—and the Trump White House—in warning that any warrant requirements would constitute 'a crippling requirement in national security and terrorism cases.'"

Just to sum up, the Democrats have helped, voted for, and often argued in favor of all of the following:

- giving Trump unlimited war powers
- giving Trump unlimited trade negotiation powers
- giving Trump unlimited surveillance powers
- giving Trump the power to lock someone up indefinitely without a trial or charges under the National Defense Authorization Act[6]
- giving Trump the power to assassinate American citizens without a trial or charges[7]
- giving Trump's administration full control of our electoral system infrastructure.[8]

If this is considered "resistance," then I don't want to be a part of it. I'd rather spend my time *resisting* the "resistance," and thereby taking this dictator's toolkit away from Donald Trump.

As George Carlin said, "It's a big club, and you ain't in it." Schiff is corrupt and working for corporate America and Wall Street. Trump is corrupt and working for corporate America and Wall Street. Ninety-five percent of the Democratic congresspeople are corrupt and working for corporate America and Wall Street. Ninety-nine percent of the Republicans are corrupt and working for corporate America and Wall Street.

Do not expect them to save us.

We cannot look to inverted totalitarianism to save us from inverted totalitarianism.[9] The ruling elite will let us die and then charge us for the coffins. We need to organize on the local level—change things in our states and cities, where it's still corrupt, but a little bit less so.

Don't wait for their permission to make a better world.

NOTES

1   Jordan Fabian, "Trump Says He Would Re-enter TPP Trade Deal If It's Made 'Substantially Better,'" The Hill, January 25, 2018, accessed September 26, 2019, http://thehill.com/homenews/administration/370715-trump-says-he-would-re-enter-tpp-trade-deal-if-its-made-substantially.

2   Jill Colvin, "Trump: The U.S. Will Stay in NAFTA and Renegotiate a Better Deal," Inc., April 27, 2017, accessed September 26, 2019, https://www.inc.com/associated-press/donald-trump-us-not-leaving-nafta.html.

3   Alexander Bolton, "Senate Approves Fast-Track, Sending Trade Bill to White House," The Hill, June 24, 2014, accessed September 26, 2019, http://thehill.com/homenews/senate/246035-senate-approves-fast-track-sending-trade-bill-to-white-house.

4   Connor O'Brien, "Senate Scuttles Rand Paul's War Powers Repeal," Politico, September 13, 2017, accessed September 26, 2019, https://www.politico.com/story/2017/09/13/war powers-aumf-rand-paul-senate-242662.

5   Glenn Greenwald, "The Same Democrats Who Denounce Donald Trump as a Lawless, Treasonous Authoritarian Just Voted to Give Him Vast Warrantless Spying Powers," Intercept, January 12, 2018, accessed September 26, 2019, https://theintercept.com/2018/01/12/the-same-democrats-who-denounce-trump-as-a-lawless-treasonous-authoritarian-just-voted-to-give-him-vast-warrantless-spying-powers/.

6   Steve Mariotti, "This Administration Now Has the Power to Indefinitely Detain Americans without Charge or Trial," HuffPost, March 27, 2017, accessed September 26, 2019, https://www.huffingtonpost.com/entry/this-administration-has-the-power-to-indefinitely-detain_us_58d919f5e4b0f633072b39be.

7   Spencer Ackerman, "US Cited Controversial Law in Decision to Kill American Citizen by Drone," Guardian, June 23, 2014, accessed

September 26, 2019, https://www.theguardian.com/world/2014/jun/23/us-justification-drone-killing-american-citizen-awlaki.

8   Katie Bo Williams, "DHS Designates Election Systems as 'Critical Infrastructure,'" The Hill, January 6, 2017, accessed September 26, 2019, http://thehill.com/policy/national-security/313132-dhs-designates-election-systems-as-critical-infrastructure.

9   Chris Hedges, "Sheldon Wolin and Inverted Totalitarianism," Truthdig, November 2, 2015, accessed September 26, 2019, https://www.truthdig.com/articles/sheldon-wolin-and-inverted-totalitarianism/.

A BRIEF DIGRESSION ON WHETHER CONSUMERISM CHANGES LOVE

I have never once had that moment when you're falling in love with someone and you're walking on a beach and you start kissing and a large wave suddenly soaks your shoes and pants up to your knee and you don't care, because you're in love. I feel like I've seen that moment in every movie, commercial, music video, and TV show I've ever watched that included even a moment of love. At least in American media, love is . . . getting your shoes and your jeans and her dress and her shoes all wet and not giving a shit. (Do they sell posters that say that?)

Yet it's never happened for me and I'm starting to worry it means I'm un-American or even inhuman. According to television, movies, and commercials, we should all have that moment when our clothes get wet, and we don't care, and somehow it represents what really matters in life. Let me be clear that I have been in love; I've been in love on a beach; I've been in love on a beach kissing the person I'm in love with when a rogue wave soaked my shoes and my jeans. I've had that proverbially magical moment. But I have to confess—a part of me still cared. In fact, most of me still cared. About the clothes, I mean. Inside my head, there were questions like, "What the fuck am I gonna do now? In about 30 seconds the 'magic' will be over, and I'll have drenched shoes for the rest of the night, not to mention the sand issue. Even if I take these off and try to rinse out the sand, I'll probably still be covered in sand. And we all know that's where blisters come from—walking around in wet, sandy shoes. Just ask the early settlers. And love can't fix blisters. And we're going to dinner after this? What do I take my shoes and socks off at the restaurant and let them air out on the seat next to me like a freak or a vagabond or an asshole looking to get a response from the other people in the restaurant? Why did we think this would be romantic? Blisters and a squishing sound as you walk are not romantic."

That's what I thought. What I said out loud was, "Ha! Who cares?!"

This makes me wonder: Are we living our lives in a genuine, authentic manner or is a large part of it subconsciously (consciously?) mimicking bullshit from movies and TV and Cialis commercials? And the people who write this crap: Are they writing the wet shoes moment because it's honestly what they believe falling in love looks like? Or is it because they saw it in a commercial 10 years earlier and internalized it? Which came first, the chicken or the chicken walking in the water worried about the sand stuck between his toes or talons or claws or whatever chickens currently have?

And if you're lucky enough to have the "true love clothing ruined on the beach" moment, even if you're enjoying it, aren't a large percentage of people thinking, "This is so cool I'm having that moment. The moment that signifies young love. I'm actually doing it! I don't even care that my clothing is getting wet." In which case, they're no longer "in" the moment. They're outside of it commenting on how awesome it is. (And I would argue a large percentage of those people are also telling themselves that in order to convince themselves it's "totes fine" that their clothing is wet.)

And then there's the cynical, morbid version of this scene in which a guy is walking on the beach alone and a wave hits, soaking his pants and shoes, and he doesn't care, because he's drowning in thoughts of his own mortality and the intense loneliness he currently feels. In both cases, no one gives a fuck about their shoes or blisters or whether some sort of algae could stain their pants forevermore. In one case, this apathy means intense love and, in the other, it means severe depression. Both cases are sold to us through media depictions as incredibly meaningful—in fact, maybe it's all that really matters in life—and, in fact, neither of them matters at all.

You could have the wet clothes moment with a woman/man/other you're deeply in love with, yet the relationship could still collapse a month later. Getting your shoes wet together does not foreshadow—or even necessarily correlate—with endless love. Whether you're willing to ruin a pair of wingtips with a young lady (fuck it, why not wingtips?) is not what decides whether your love lasts. In fact, a better indicator is probably whether you remember to take your wingtips off when you walk into the apartment. If you leave your shoes on despite his/her endless pleading that you fucking take them off, then your relationship is probably destined to fail. Or if you do take off your shoes but then she/he just finds something else you're doing wrong and this goes on forever until you're a broken human being—that is also a better indicator of a doomed love. But they never portray that moment in the movies/TV shows/boner pill ads, because it wouldn't look romantic. It would be true but look rather pathetic. Sometimes real life looks pathetic—it just does. Sometimes true love looks lame but means the world.

The same goes for true depression and existential angst. It's probably not wet socks that really prove it. It's more likely to be unwashed socks that really prove it—a pile of completely odious socks that have gone unwashed for weeks. That is what depression more often looks like.

So are we just living these moments in a Sisyphean effort to feel the love we saw in that film? Or maybe we're naturally living those moments, but we give them more import because of their "celebrity" status. And then when that kissing moment doesn't live up to the hype (maybe because you're not in love but more likely because you're worried about your socks), it will inevitably depress you that you didn't feel what you thought you should. Then, once depressed, you'll have to go back and traverse the shallow waves alone—because that's what depressed people do to demonstrate their desperation.

DEBUNKING THE *WASHINGTON POST'S* LIES AS THEY DEBUNK DONALD TRUMP'S 1,950 LIES

The *Washington Post* put out an in-depth analysis of President Trump's 1,950 lies and misleading claims over his first year in office.[1] It's an impressive feat since the *Post* had to fact-check everything and allow Trump's third-grade-level speeches to enter its fact-checkers' ear holes, a punishment I wouldn't wish on my worst enemies.

The writers at the *Washington Post* are correct that lies spray out of Trump's face with the force of an untethered fire hose. They're also correct that almost every statement by Trump is either false or misleading. However, the irony is that almost every statement the *Washington Post* prints in correcting Trump's lies is in itself a lie or misleading statement. So, to be clear, I'm not saying Trump is not lying. I'm saying that the way that our mainstream media correct him is also meant to deceive us.

The *Washington Post* starts with December and counts backward through the year. Here are my corrections to its corrections to Trump's lies. (This is only a few weeks' worth, but you'll probably get my gist and need to purge yourself in a bathroom immediately.)

Trump statement: "If the Dems (Crooked Hillary) got elected, your stocks would be down 50% from values on Election Day. Now they have a great future—and just beginning!"

Washington Post correction: "Trump of course has no idea how stocks would have performed if Clinton had won the election. The stock market rise in Trump's first year was a continuation of a bull market that started under President Obama—and was mirrored by worldwide securities markets. The U.S. rise in 2017 was not unique. When looking at the Standard & Poor's 500 stock index, it's clear U.S. stocks haven't rallied as robustly as their foreign equivalents."

Trump statement: "The stock market is at an all-time high and continues to go up, up, up."

Washington Post correction: "This is a flip-flop for Trump. Before he was elected, he dismissed the stock-market performance under Obama as 'artificial' and 'a bubble.' Moreover, the U.S. rise in 2017 was not unique. When looking at the Standard & Poor's 500 stock index, it's clear U.S. stocks haven't rallied as robustly as their foreign equivalents."

What the *Post* won't tell you is that the stock market does great when workers are effectively exploited. When the average American worker doesn't have the power or leverage to demand better pay or safer working conditions, corporations are thrilled, the stock market grows, and the fabled coke-fueled Wall Street parties go off without a hitch. The market has also continued to grow with increasing inequality. Furthermore, over 90 percent of the income gains since the 2008 collapse have gone to the top 1 percent, and 80 percent of stock value overall is held by the top 10 percent of the population.[2]

Plus, the market does not take into account externalities such as impacts on the environment. Even as the environment collapses around us, the stock market thrives.

So while Trump is lying to us about what the stock market would've done under President Hillary, the *Washington Post* is lying to us about the nature of the stock market (as is Trump). The *Post* acts as if Wall Street's growth is somehow good for average Americans. It's not. Trump, Hillary, and the *Post* are all part of an elite class enjoying the spoils of a fully exploited working class. Judging the health of our society by looking at stock prices is like judging the health of a dying man by looking at the leeches on his skin. "Wow, those leeches are very happy. This man is in peak condition!"

Trump statement: "I use Social Media not because I like to, but because it is the only way to fight a *very* dishonest and unfair 'press,' now often referred to as Fake News Media. Phony and non-existent 'sources' are being used more often than ever. Many stories & reports a pure fiction!"

***Washington Post* correction:** "Trump tends to deem negative articles as 'fake news' even if they are accurate. Mainstream news organizations can certainly make mistakes, or rely on sources who are inaccurate, but they do not use nonexistent sources or print 'pure fiction.'"

This almost needs no response, because most people know how ridiculous it is. Of course, Trump lies endlessly. He hardly knows how to speak an honest sentence. (After all, he's a barely literate man who called himself "a genius" just a couple of days ago.) But the idea that the *Washington Post*, long known to put out propaganda for the CIA and other government agencies, is somehow free of intentionally misleading the American public is laughable on a level that would put the new Dave Chappelle special to shame.

One need look no further than its hilarious "Prop or Not" article (which was quickly debunked) to see how far down bullshit lane it's willing to travel.[3] But more importantly, what the *Post* won't tell us here is what it won't tell us all the rest of the time. (And that last sentence is not a typo.) The corporate media—even when it's getting the story correct—is endlessly avoiding certain topics or points.

Just last week, former *New York Times* reporter James Risen revealed how he was stopped by his editors from reporting on the Bush-era illegal surveillance of American citizens.[4] That occurred a decade before the Edward Snowden revelations and could have changed the outcome of presidential elections as well as the course of our government's continued assault on our civil liberties. (No biggie.)

Our media avoids everything from climate change (which it has known about for decades but hardly covers even as it covers extreme weather events)[5] to the current US-backed destruction of Yemen to the fact that only 1 percent of terror plots stopped by the FBI are real—and most of those, 99 percent, were helped along by the FBI.[6] (To add anecdotal evidence to my point, my friend Abby Martin and I have both forced the *New York Times* to issue corrections in the past year on statements about us that a simple Google search could have proven wrong.)

Trump statement: "Since the election we have created more than 2 million jobs."

Washington Post **correction:** Trump is counting jobs from Election Day, even though he did not take office until almost three months later. At the time, about 1.7 million jobs had been created during his presidency."

Trump statement: "Unemployment is at a 17-year low."

Washington Post **correction:** "This is flip flop for Trump. While campaigning Trump dismissed the unemployment rate as made up, suggesting unemployment was closer to 30 or 40 percent. Since becoming president Trump has embraced the figure."

Shouldn't it matter in the "correction" that most of the jobs created are part-time and low-paid? About 25 percent of those in our country with part-time jobs currently live in poverty.[7] This is not Trump's fault but an ongoing trend in America's late-stage capitalist economy that is exploiting nearly everyone more and more. Trump's economic team is filled with people from Goldman Sachs and Citibank, just as Obama's was. (Many people don't even know that Citigroup chose almost all of Obama's cabinet.)[8] Wall Street has captured our government and therefore does whatever is good for the top 1 percent who rule Wall Street.

On top of that, technology will soon replace most jobs, and we need to adjust to a nearly jobless society. Studies show roughly 50 percent of jobs in the US could be replaced by artificial intelligence in the next 20 years.[9] And, in fact, the percentage might be much higher than that, seeing as technology advances exponentially—whereas we humans seem to be devolving tenaciously.

So acting as if poorly paid part-time job creation is the only way to judge success as a president is ignorant or manipulative on a level usually reserved for the cast of *Survivor*. Even our "most successful" corporations hardly pay their employees—Amazon was just added to the list of major corporations with a significant number of employees on food stamps.[10] The *Washington Post* wants the struggling American worker to remain unaware of what's coming and of the power we could all have if we knew what to demand from a government that is hypothetically supposed to work for us.

Trump statement: "Congress has authorized funding at near-record levels so that we can rebuild our full military might after years of dangerous cuts and depletion of our military."
Washington Post **correction:** "Trump, perhaps because he is reading his weekly address from a script, is more careful than usual. He does not claim a record level of spending and he notes that it is 'authorized,' as Congress must still appropriate funds. Still, Trump claims the military has been depleted due to years of budget cuts, but the decreased military budget reflects the close of two wars: the war in Iraq and the war in Afghanistan. Despite the decreased budget, the total budget is still larger than it was in 2000, before either war began."

Here, the *Post* is bragging about military spending while failing to mention that our military spending is out of control on all levels. We spend more on our military than the next eight countries combined.[11] At the same time, we refuse to fund universal health care, infrastructure projects, paid maternity leave, and education. Last week in Baltimore, children sat in freezing classrooms, because the schools didn't have money for heating.[12] While even the *Post* covered the Baltimore story, it won't ever connect such an issue to our utterly psychotic military spending. Part of how our corporate media manufactures consent for our illogical and highly immoral system is by leaving everything out of context, intentionally avoiding connecting the dots. The United Nations estimated it would take 30 billion dollars a year to end world hunger, and then in 2015 increased that number to 267 billion dollars.[13] Even if the correct figure is 267 billion dollars, that's still less than half of the over 600 billion dollars we spend on "defense."

If we wanted it to be defense, why don't we pay to end world hunger, at which point we would be the safest country in the world, because no one would want to bomb the country that ended world hunger. Or we can continue to listen to the *Post* haggle with Donald Trump as to whether or not he's built up our "depleted" military.

Oh yeah, I almost forgot: the *Post* acts as if the wars in Iraq and Afghanistan are over even though about 40 thousand people were killed in Iraq in 2017,[14] and we still have at least 11 thousand troops in Afghanistan.[15] But how does one declare a war is "over" when it was never really a war to begin with—but, rather, an ongoing assault on a population, designed to maintain endless instability in a region and allow the US to hold on to our global empire?

The *Post* misses tiny insignificant facts like that.

Trump statement: "I'm the one that saved coal. I'm the one that created jobs. You know West Virginia is doing fantastically now."

Washington Post **correction:** West Virginia's GDP increased 3 percent in the first quarter of 2017. The recent bump is due in part to the increased price of metallurgic coal, which is used to make steel, and a price increase in natural gas exports. West Virginia produces roughly 5 percent of the natural gas in the U.S. and as the price of natural gas rises, the demand for coal increases, spurring growth in the state. Trump can't take credit for the change in prices, which fluctuate with market forces. As for 'saving coal,' there has barely been any job growth in the coal industry since Trump became president. According to the Bureau of Labor statistics, only 900 jobs have been created in the coal industry since Trump became president—an increase of less than 3 percent."

The *Post* corrects Trump's assertion that coal jobs have returned to West Virginia. However, it doesn't mention that coal is the dirtiest of all fuels and, therefore, is helping to send our planet down a death spiral of greenhouse gases.[16] Something tells me most of its readers might like to know there won't be a world for their grandkids to grow up in. We should all be wildly celebrating the move away from coal in an orgiastic manner.

The *Post*'s correction is the equivalent of the president bragging that he brought hit man jobs back to West Virginia and then the *Post* saying: "In fact, hit man jobs have not returned as promised, and very few people have been professionally murdered in West Virginia in the past year." The *Post* should have said: "In fact, coal jobs have not returned, and that is a good thing if we value the air in our lungs and the life in our bodies."

Trump statement: "Now that the individual mandate is officially killed, people have no idea how big a deal that was. It's the most unpopular part of Obamacare. But now, Obamacare is essentially. . . You know, you saw this. . . . It's basically dead over a period of time."

Washington Post **correction:** "While the individual mandate was an important incentive for Americans to seek health insurance, it was only one part of a far-reaching law that remains intact. The repeal does not take effect until 2019, and enrollment in Obamacare has remained strong. The Congressional Budget Office says the marketplaces are expected to remain stable for years."

What the *Washington Post* won't mention is that the US is the only developed country without universal health care. And Obamacare was written by the health insurance industry (initially introduced by the GOP in the 1990s). This is an industry that by definition profits most when people are least taken care of. This doesn't mean it isn't great that more people have coverage than before Obamacare, but, rather, it's pathetic that one of the richest countries in the world doesn't cover everyone to begin with. That context might help in any correction on this issue.

Trump statement: "We see the drugs pouring into the country, we need the wall."
***Washington Post* correction:** "The wall will have virtually no effect on drugs coming into the country. According to reports by the DEA, the majority of drugs are smuggled through legal ports of entry or smuggled through underground tunnels.

Whoa, whoa, whoa. If the *Post* really wants to correct Trump, it would mention that the catastrophic drug war is a war on our own people and was designed from the beginning to arrest black people and activists.[17] Furthermore, in Portugal, where drugs have been decriminalized and are treated as a health problem, instead of a crime problem, illicit drug use has decreased and so have overdoses.[18] No so-called "correction" of Trump's ridiculous statement that a wall will stop drug use is even remotely complete without talking about the context of the drug war. And here's the thing—The *Washington Post* knows this.

It knows everything I just stated. It's even covered some of it in the past. Yet most of the time it leaves out this context, so that our nation continues arresting thousands upon thousands of people (of color) a year for small-time drug use. It seems the *Post* wants to have its coke and eat it too.

Overall, The *Washington Post* has filled its "corrections" with decontextualized manipulations of its own. (And I've covered only about two weeks out of 52.) The *Post* is lying to us as much as Trump is. Until we can see these issues for what they really are, we will never be able to change anything.

NOTES

1   Glenn Kessler, Meg Kelly, and Nicole Lewis, "President Trump Has Made 1,950 False or Misleading Claims over 347 Days," *Washington Post*, January 2, 2018, accessed September 26, 2019, https://www.washingtonpost.com/news/fact-checker/wp/2018/01/02/president-trump-has-made-1949-false-or-misleading-claims-over-347-days/?utm_term=.1558cc90d51f.

2   Bryce Covert, "The 1 Percent Have Gotten All the Income Gains from the Recovery," Think Progress, January 28, 2015, accessed September 26, 2019, https://thinkprogress.org/the-1-percent-have-gotten-all-the-income-gains-from-the-recovery-6bee14aab1/.

3   Ben Norton and Glenn Greenwald, "Washington Post Disgracefully Promotes a McCarthyite Blacklist from a New, Hidden, and Very Shady Group," Intercept, November 26, 2016, accessed September 26, 2019, https://theintercept.com/2016/11/26/washington-post-disgracefully-promotes-a-mccarthyite-blacklist-from-a-new-hidden-and-very-shady-group/.

4   James Risen, "My Life as a *New York Times* Reporter in the Shadow of the War on Terror," Intercept, January 3, 2018, accessed September 26, 2019, https://theintercept.com/2018/01/03/my-life-as-a-new-york-times-reporter-in-the-shadow-of-the-war-on-terror/.

5   Jake Johnson, "Corporate Media 'Failed' to Connect 2017's Extreme Weather to Climate Crisis: Study," Common Dreams, January 5, 2018, accessed September 26, 2019, https://www.commondreams.org/news/2018/01/05/corporate-media-failed-connect-2017s-extreme-weather-climate-crisis-study.

6   Joshua Holland, "Only 1 Percent of 'Terrorists' Caught by the FBI Are Real," Salon, July 10, 2013, accessed September 26, 2019, https://www.salon.com/2013/07/10/only_1_percent_of_terrorists_caught_by_fbi_are_real_partner/.

7   Patrick Gillespie, "America's Part-Time Workforce Is Huge," CNN, April 25, 2016, accessed September 26, 2019, http://money.cnn.com/2016/04/25/news/economy/part-time-jobs/index.html.

8   Redacted Tonight, "JAW-DROPPING Leak Proves Big Banks Completely Control Our Government," YouTube, November 7, 2016, accessed September 26, 2019, https://www.youtube.com/watch?v=dEKxU8nlyoc&feature=youtu.be&t=43s.

9   Marguerite Ward, "AI and Robots Could Threaten Your Career within 5 Years," CNBC, October 5, 2017, accessed September 26, 2019, https://www.cnbc.com/2017/10/05/report-ai-and-robots-could-change-your-career-within-5-years.html.

10   Mark Williams, "Amazon Makes List of Large Companies with Workers Receiving Food Stamps," *Columbus Dispatch*, January 5, 2018, accessed September 26, 2019, http://www.dispatch.com/news/20180105/amazon-makes-list-of-large-companies-with-workers-receiving-food-stamps.

11   Lauren Carroll, "Obama: US Spends More on Military than Next 8 Nations Combined," Politifact, January 13, 2016, accessed September 26, 2019, http://www.politifact.com/truth-o-meter/statements/2016/jan/13/barack-obama/obama-us-spends-more-military-next-8-nations-combi/.

12   Madison Park, Jason Hanna, Paul Murphy, and Sheena Jones, "Baltimore Closes Public Schools after Students Sat in Cold Classrooms," CNN, January 4, 2018, accessed September 26, 2019, http://www.cnn.com/2018/01/04/us/baltimore-schools-cold/index.html.

13   Joseph D'Urso, "How Much Would It Cost to End Hunger?" World Economic Forum, July 16, 2015, accessed September 26, 2019, https://www.weforum.org/agenda/2015/07/how-much-would-it-cost-to-end-hunger/.

14   Antiwar.com, "War of Terror: Nearly 40,000 Killed in Iraq During 2017," MintPress News, January 2, 2018, accessed September 26, 2019, http://www.mintpressnews.com/war-terror-nearly-40000-killed-iraq-2017/235984/.

15   Helene Cooper, "US Says It Has 11,000 Troops in Afghanistan, More than Formerly Disclosed," *New York Times*, August 30, 2017, accessed September 26, 2019, https://www.nytimes.com/2017/08/30/world/asia/afghanistan-troop-totals.html?_r=0.

16   Eleanor Goldfield, "Humans Only Have a Few Decades Left: But There Might Be a Way to Change That," Lee Camp Official Website, January 9, 2018, accessed September 26, 2019, https://leecamp.com/humans-decades-left-might-way-change/.

17   Tim March, "Richard Nixon Used America's 'War on Drugs' as Excuse to Target 'Anti-War Left and Black People,' Claims Former Aide," *Independent*, March 23, 2016, accessed September 26, 2019, http://www.independent.co.uk/news/world/americas/richard-nixon-used-america-s-war-on-drugs-as-excuse-to-target-anti-war-left-and-black-people-claims-a6948521.html.

18   Lauren Frayer, "In Portugal, Drug Use Is Treated as a Medical Issue, Not a Crime," NPR, April 18, 2017, accessed September 26, 2019, https://www.npr.org/sections/parallels/2017/04/18/524380027/in-portugal-drug-use-is-treated-as-a-medical-issue-not-a-crime.

HOW TO WRITE PROPAGANDA FOR THE *NEW YORK TIMES*, AS SEEN IN AN ATTACK PIECE ON ME

Dear reader, after my response to the New York Times came out, the Times made multiple retractions to their initial article about me. Of course, they still left the rest of the lie-riddled piece up online. One can only assume they refuse to take it down because too much honesty would ruin their reputation.

This past Thursday the *New York Times* vomited up a hit piece on little ol' me[1]—a guy who has been doing stand-up comedy for nearly 20 years and thought maybe that comedy could be used to inform and inspire audiences, rather than just to make fun of the differences between men and women.

At first, when you're the center of a smear job, you're annoyed and frustrated. But as I read further through the piece, I realized it was a master class in how to write propaganda for one of the most "respected" news outlets in our country. I'm actually grateful it was written about me, because now I can see with my own eyes exactly how the glorious chicanery is done. I count no less than 15 lies, manipulations, and false implications in this short article, a score that even our fearless prevaricator in chief Donald Trump would envy.

So here now is a "how-to" for writing propaganda for the *New York Times*—using the smear piece against me as an example.

Step One: Prime the Readers

The author Jason Zinoman starts the piece this way:

> Last week, Lee Camp, an acerbic left-wing comic, dedicated six minutes of his topical TV show, "Redacted Tonight," to the discredited conspiracy theory that it wasn't Russian hackers who leaked emails during the presidential election but Seth Rich, the Democratic National Committee staff member killed in a botched robbery.

Okay, folks, we're off to the races. Now what does one take from that opening paragraph?

I bet you assumed that this crank, Lee Camp, did a segment bolstering a discredited nonsense theory about the death of DNC staffer Seth Rich. But in fact, the segment I performed on-air does nothing but cast doubts on the theory that Seth Rich was murdered for the leaked emails. You can watch the segment on YouTube and judge for yourself.[2]

Zinoman does go on in the next paragraph to say "Mr. Camp's tepid take—he doesn't know the truth, but he's skeptical." So, despite Zinoman's sheepish second-paragraph admission that I didn't back the conspiracy theory, he's already made use of a nice little psychological trick called "priming." His opening paragraph has primed the reader to believe I give credence to discredited conspiracy theories. That, along with the title of the article—"An American Comic on a Russian Channel: What He Avoids Speaks Volumes"—has set the reader up to believe that I'm a Russian agent of sorts putting forward conspiracies, and our brave Ivy League author has been able to spot my sinister plot. (Thank god he was here or the plot might very well have destroyed America!) And, in fact, Zinoman goes on to reference the Seth Rich segment multiple times as if I had supported the theories.

That brings us to our next propaganda trick. . .

Step Two: Guilt by Association

That Mr. Camp does this on RT—which describes itself as the "Russian view on global news" and which paid Michael T. Flynn, the former national security adviser, to speak at the gala where he sat next to Vladimir V. Putin—raises questions about the comedian's independence, particularly when he delves into the conspiracy about Mr. Rich. Just last month, Andrew Feinberg, a former White House reporter for Sputnik, another Russian-financed media outlet, said that his bosses "wanted the Seth Rich story pushed."

So now he's somehow looping in me and my comedy news show with Michael Flynn, Putin, Sputnik (the radio channel), Seth Rich conspiracies, and I'm pretty sure he mentioned something about me hanging out with Bill Cosby.

Here's the problem with that paragraph—I have nothing to do with Sputnik. I have nothing to do with Michael Flynn, Andrew Feinberg, or Vladimir Putin. I have never spoken to or met any of them (nor do I speak Russian, so a conversation with Putin would consist of me grunting and trying to act out references to The Hunt for Red October). I have never been told by anyone at RT America to say anything about Seth Rich nor have I seen anyone being told to talk about Seth Rich nor did my segment even support the theory that he was killed by the DNC.

Nothing in that paragraph has anything to do with me, but Zinoman wants to lead you to believe it does. This technique is called "guilt by association," although Zinoman couldn't actually find the "association" part, so he just included a paragraph about these people to imply guilt by association. Subconsciously the reader is left to think, "If Lee Camp didn't have anything to do with any of those things, then our fearless author would never have brought any of it up."

Furthermore, Zinoman is correct that RT has said in the past that they are "the Russian view on global news" in the same way BBC has said in the past that they are "the British view of global news." However, BBC also creates many shows that are outside the realm of straight news—such as *Dr. Who*. I've rarely heard anyone accuse *Dr. Who* of being the British view of global news. (Why do those crazy Brits always insist on taking flying police boxes to travel anywhere?)

My show, written by me and my correspondents, is certainly not the Russian view of global news and neither is—for example—Larry King's show on RT America. (I get that *Dr. Who* is further afield of news than my show is, but the analogy is simply meant to say these networks create shows that are not strictly straight news.) And anyone who thinks CNN, for instance, isn't the American view of global news is kidding themselves. But I have to agree that CNN's *Anthony Bourdain: Parts Unknown* did a terrible job of covering the terror attacks in London.

I speak only for my show—I don't speak for any other show on RT America. I write the words I say on *Redacted Tonight* and have never been told I have to say anything. Compare that to . . . (Oh, so many examples to choose from! How can I only pick one?!) . . . let's say, Melissa Harris Perry on MSNBC. After being forced out, she said she was censored often.[3] As an example, she said—close to showtime—that she was told not to cover Beyoncé's Black Panther–inspired Super Bowl halftime show. In no uncertain terms MSNBC heads stopped her from talking about it. Perry was literally forbidden from discussing the two most popular things to ever exist on our planet Earth—Beyoncé and the Super Bowl (and I'm including food and sex).

Now that we've established a good foundation of guilt by association (without the association) and some priming and some baseless implications, it's time to move on to. . .

Step Three: Write Off Good Attributes That Don't Fit the Storyline

> Mr. Camp's hard-edge critique of corporate greed and American policy is genuine; he was taking this line in his stand-up act before working for RT. But context matters.

Writing about the fact that I have spent two decades involved in comedy, much of it political, much of it trying to make America better, trying to stand up for people over profit . . . well, that just wouldn't fit with the author's theme. So he had to find a way to get this stumbling block out of the way of his race to propaganda victory! He did that by casually mentioning the good attributes before writing them off as meaningless. My work and what I stand for is beside the point, because "context matters."

Step Four: It's What the Person Doesn't Say That Really Matters

Because Zinoman wasn't able to find any statements from me pledging allegiance to Russia or supporting war by Russia (or anyone for that matter) or even voicing support for Donald Trump in any way, shape, or form (because none of those statements exist), he had to resort to going after what I *don't* say. . . . And oddly, I agree with him that what people don't say can be important, but we'll get to that in a moment.

> As hacking and Russia's relationship to the Trump campaign increasingly dominate headlines, Mr. Camp's refusal to dig into the story is conspicuous. He avoids the subject on air, and while he does criticize President Trump, his considerable comic bile rarely focuses on him.

Despite all his extensive research (sarcasm), Jason Zinoman failed to read the title of my show, *Redacted Tonight*. I'm hoping he knows what the word "tonight" means, but maybe the "redacted" part eluded him. "Redacted" means "censored," and my show tries very hard to focus on the news that (ironically in this conversation) is not being covered by the mainstream media, the stuff that is being censored. As he just admitted, bullshit about Trump and hacking claims fill the mainstream airwaves. Some of it true, some of it not, but all of it covered intensively. I have no interest in being a mainstream media or government mouthpiece for anyone—which is why I created REDACTED Tonight. It's also why the things I say (particularly the anti-corporate things) are not allowed on any standard American TV channel. Zinoman, on the other hand, is quite content working at a propaganda outlet like the New York Times—more on that later—and, after all, context matters.

Zinoman tepidly says "while he does criticize Trump his considerable comic bile rarely focuses on him." Well, first of all, for anyone who watches my show regularly, you know that hardly an episode goes by in which I don't call Trump a mega-lomaniacal fascist man-boy with the decision-making capacity of a gopher recently run over by a Hummer (or something similar). You can watch numerous examples on YouTube.[4] In fact I went harsher on Trump than pretty much all of the mainstream media during the campaign season. Please point to the moments when Anderson Cooper or Brian Williams called Trump a fascist or a psychopath or photoshopped his head onto Hitler's body. (I did all those things.)

And the reason I don't spend *even more* lengthy segments on him is: A) we're the "redacted" stories, remember? The title of my show is not "Stories Everyone Has Heard 8 Billion Times on Cable News . . . Tonight"; B) I don't believe Trump is the cause of our country's main problems. I believe he is a symptom of an incredibly corrupt corporate-ruled system. He is a horrible and rather—not bright—man, but he is not the cause of the millions of hungry and homeless and impris-oned in our country. He is not the cause of the flaws in our democracy and our media. He is just the pimple that has risen up. So either Zinoman is intentionally misunderstanding the viewpoint of my show, or he's just so desperate to push his talking points that he's looking past it.

And I believe the *New York Times* is one of those directly responsible for making Trump president by—along with other mainstream outlets—giving him 5 billion dollars of free coverage during the campaign season.[5] In fact, Bernie Sanders supporters got so angry with the *Times* for their lack of coverage that the *Times* eventually issued a response.[6] Even in that response, in which they say they've covered Sanders plenty, they admit that in one sample month Sanders had 14 articles about him while Trump had 63 articles. If that distribution of coverage had been *anywhere near* balanced, we would have either Bernie Sanders or Hillary Clinton as president. So, Mr. Zinoman, let me know when you'd like to apologize for your outlet giving us the Trump presidency.

Step Five: Fuck It, Insult the Guy's Looks

> Mr. Camp—who looks like a Broadway musical costume designer's idea of a counterculture comedian, with "Jesus Christ Superstar" hair and T-shirts bearing images of Bill Hicks or "Catch-22". . .

The *New York Times* has so deeply fallen into their own propaganda hole, they've resorted to just insulting the looks of people they feel threatened by. I don't know what Jason Zinoman looks like, but I'm sure it's awesome.

Step Six: Trot Out Discredited Neocon Think Tank–Backed Source

> Liz Wahl is a former journalist for RT who quit on air, accusing the network of "whitewashing the actions of Putin" in its coverage of the Russian invasion of Ukraine. Ms. Wahl calls Mr. Camp a "stooge." . . . Ms. Wahl was working at RT when "Redacted Tonight"

had its premiere in 2014, and she recalled that it was envisioned in the style of "The Daily Show."

There's only one problem with this statement. . . . It's not true.

Liz Wahl was not working at RT America when *Redacted Tonight* premiered.

Liz Wahl quit on March 5, 2014. *Redacted Tonight* first aired at the end of May 2014. So, you know, at least Wahl and Zinoman were only about three months off.

But I can't blame Zinoman for not catching something that Wahl incorrectly described, since doing so would've required at least one—if not two—Wikipedia searches. (Who has the time??) Egregious mistakes like this don't just speak to the sloppy work of the author, they also speak to his eagerness to portray me and my show in a certain light. He seems to have thought, "If I can't find someone who has an inside track on how *Redacted Tonight* is secretly sinister, I'll pretend I do."

But besides that, Liz Wahl's claims about how and why she left RT America have been completely debunked, including in this Truthdig article titled "How Cold War–Hungry Neocons Stage Managed RT Anchor Liz Wahl's Resignation." It details how the Foreign Policy Initiative (FPI) was in fact tweeting about Wahl's on-air resignation before it ever happened, and they had had a long-standing relationship with her. The authors say:

> The tweets from FPI suggested a direct level of coordination between Wahl and the neoconservative think tank. . . . Launched by Weekly Standard founder William Kristol and two former foreign policy aides to Mitt Romney, Dan Senor and Robert Kagan (the husband of Assistant Secretary of State for European and Eurasian Affairs Victoria Nuland), FPI grew directly out of the Project for a New American Century that led the public pressure campaign for a unilateral

U.S. invasion of Iraq after the Bin Laden–orchestrated 9/11 attacks.[7]

So a completely discredited source gave Jason Zinoman the incorrect statements he was looking for. This is not the only time in recent months the *New York Times* has been caught flat-out lying about such things. In fact, former RT host Abby Martin issued a response to the fake news put out about her.[8] Apparently the *Times* is just tripping over themselves to push this propaganda, so much so that they can't or won't verify simple facts.

Zinoman doesn't let any of this stop him from quoting Wahl in the article. He's hoping you won't learn these things about her and her past. But, you know . . . context matters.

Step Seven: Lie
Enough beating around the bush, it's time to flat-out lie.

> According to several people in the comedy scene, his stand-up diatribes succeeded with like-minded fans but had more trouble with crowds that didn't share his point of view. "We wouldn't book him for a weekend, let's put it that way," said Cris Italia, one of the owners of the New York comedy club the Stand.

First of all, I'd love to know who these mysterious "comedy scene" people were. Waitresses? Busboys? *Phantom of the Opera* types lurking underneath the stage silently judging my satire? Unfortunately, we'll never know because "the comedy scene" only speak in deep cover. (First rule of comedy scene—don't talk about comedy scene!)

Second, Zinoman claims that Cris Italia told him that the comedy club the Stand in New York City would not book me on the weekends. Cris had actually contacted me two days before the *Times* article came out to tell me that a reporter had reached out to him about me, and that he could tell from the questions the reporter was trying to portray me in a negative light (read:

trying to push an agenda rather than being, you know, a journalist). Italia said: "I told him you were liked by everyone. I also said what Dennis Miller, Janeane Garofalo, and Marc Maron were for their generation, you were for this generation."

But Zinoman did the smart thing for a propaganda machine—leave out the stuff that does not fit the false story you're pushing. (I picture Zinoman cringing on the other end of the line as nice things are said about the unscrupulous Russian agent—Lee Camp. After jotting down the quote about Dennis Miller, he furiously rips the page out of his notebook, chews it up, and swallows it.)

Cris Italia says he was next asked whether the Stand would book me on a Saturday, and he replied that they don't book headliners on weekends. (Most New York City clubs do what's called a "showcase" in which many comics get onstage over the course of the evening.) Zinoman—upon not getting the quote he wanted—must have figured he could slant this into something saying the Stand would not book me. He either didn't understand Italia or chose to misquote him. So Zinoman is sloppy at best and a fraud at worst.

Final Step: Leave the Reader with the Same (False) Prime You Started With

The article wraps up by describing my live stand-up performance at the Cutting Room in New York City a few weeks ago. Zinoman attended the show and in the article wrongly states that I performed with two correspondents from *Redacted Tonight*. Only one of the openers—John F. O'Donnell—is from *Redacted*. But getting that fact correct would have required *another* Google search. (The work never ends!) Zinoman of course fails to mention in his description:

- The 250-capacity room was nearly sold out with excited fans.
- The show went great, and I think everyone left having had a wonderful time.

- My stand-up performances (unless done for a TV special) have no connection to RT America at all. They are my own events. But the author leaves all of that out even though . . . context matters.

Anyway, the article ends like this: "Once Mr. Camp finished and the crowd had filed out, I lingered for a minute on the sidewalk. And while there wasn't any rally, I couldn't help noticing two beefy guys speaking in Russian and laughing uproariously."

What Zinoman really, *really* doesn't want you to know is that those "beefy Russians" were almost certainly not there for my stand-up comedy show. The Cutting Room had a show starting after mine that had nothing to do with my show. And guess what—that show was a rapper named Noize, who is described as "the most outspoken, daring, and exciting Russian rapper." That's right, the reason there were people in line speaking Russian outside my comedy show is because they were there to see a Russian rapper who had nothing to do with me.

And don't forget . . . context matters.

Either Zinoman knew about the rapper and decided not to reveal it (so he's basically a liar), or he didn't bother to look at the massive sign listing the performances nor ask the Russians (who probably spoke English) why they were there (in which case he's possibly the worst "journalist" to walk the earth). It's tough to say which one of those two possibilities is worse.

But describing those laughing Russians serves a purpose greater than an interesting tidbit. Zinoman sat through an entire 90-minute stand-up comedy show in which I covered everything from how our leaders force us into endless war through how we can feed every human on the planet and how we are sold an infinite parade of lies to how my comedy doesn't go over well at children's birthday parties. He saw me cover all those important issues. He saw an audience of over 200 people loving it and coming up to meet me afterwards.

He saw a guy who has fought hard for 20 years to do stand-up comedy that matters—that enlightens and informs and entertains. He saw it all. But none of that fit with the propaganda he needed to push. In fact, it went against the storyline he was trying to create.

So instead he leaves the reader with the idea that either:

- my show is meant for burly Russians (according to online analytics, roughly 80–90 percent of my viewers are Americans);
- my show is being watched over by burly Russians to make sure I don't say anything "out of line." Both of those are fake news. The reality is that burly Russians like a rapper named Noize.

I want to conclude with a little bit of context about the *New York Times* and how they've become such a propaganda outlet that they would even hire journalists who pump out loads of fake news like this article on me.

Chris Hedges worked for 15 years as a foreign correspondent at the *Times* and won a Pulitzer for his work. He now hosts the show *On Contact* at RT America. He once said of his former employer:

> [M]any at the paper have no real moral compass. They know the rules imposed by the paper's stylebook. They know what constitutes a "balanced" story. They know what the institution demands. They work hard. They have ingested the byzantine quirks and traditions of the paper. But they cannot finally make independent moral choices. The entire paper—I speak as someone who was there at the time—enthusiastically served as a propaganda machine for the impending invasion of Iraq.

Hedges went on to say, "[The senior editors] do not question the utopian faith in globalization. They support preemptive war, at least before it goes horribly wrong. And they accept unfettered capitalism, despite what it has done to the nation, as a kind of natural law."[9]

The *Times* was a strong cheerleader for the War in Iraq. (Don't worry though—they still have reporters out there looking for the weapons of mass destruction. . . . Any day now.) When Hedges came out against the Iraq War, the paper reprimanded him for "public remarks that could undermine public trust in the paper's impartiality."[10] Basically, they said, "Either stand behind this flawed, illegal invasion of Iraq or else you're not welcome at the *Times*." Hedges left the paper soon after.

Want some more evidence of exactly how the *New York Times* operates? Read world-renowned political philosopher Noam Chomsky's article from 2015 going through a single issue of the *Times* and explaining how each headline is pure propaganda.[11]

Best-selling journalist Greg Palast (BBC, *Rolling Stone*) wrote to me after he saw the article. Here's his unsolicited opinion:

> The hatchet job on Lee Camp by the NY *Times* is the pathetic new Red-baiting 2.0. The *Times* man claimed Lee was afraid to attack Trump because that would displease the owners of RT. Really? What in Lee's statement, "Fuck Trump," sounds like an endorsement?

So the next time you're reading so-called journalism in the *New York Times*, remember . . . context matters.

NOTES

1   Jason Zinoman, "An American Comic on a Russian Channel: What He Avoids Speaks Volumes," *New York Times*, June 7, 2017, accessed September 26, 2019, https://www.nytimes.com/2017/06/07/arts/television/trump-russia-comedy-redacted-tonight-lee-camp.html?mcubz=0.

2   Redacted Tonight, "The Uncomfortable TRUTH about Seth Rich," YouTube, June 2, 2017, accessed September 26, 2019, https://www.youtube.com/watch?v=u1VW1z9W5iQ.

3 Free Speech TV, "Melissa Harris-Perry on MSNBC Fallout, Race, Media, and the Presidential Race," YouTube, April 7, 2016, accessed September 26, 2019, https://www.youtube.com/watch?v=ghTrLoMC3WY.

4 Examples from the Redacted Tonight YouTube channel include: "Donald Trump: There's a Lot You Don't Know About Him," July 20, 2015, https://www.youtube.com/watch?v=5gN9VqoDGJA; "Trump Is the Final Step in the Decades-Long Corporate Criminal Takeover," December 10, 2016, https://www.youtube.com/watch?v=c4rZBwCGpvg; "Trump's Memo to the Dept. of Energy Has Caused CHAOS," December, 17, 2016, https://www.youtube.com/watch?v=bnWzIfSirdA; "WEB EXCLUSIVE: Billionaire CEO Slips Up, Reveals TRUTH About Trump Gov't," January 2, 2017, https://www.youtube.com/watch?v=ktYdU45K7-8; "Why the Media Is to Blame for Donald Trump!," January 4, 2017, https://www.youtube.com/watch?v=xZv7TmPaUiM; " "Trump Is Refilling The Swamp With Monsters & The Dems Let Him," January 22, 2017, https://www.youtube.com/watch?v=a-_INi-TKoM; all accessed September 26, 2019.

5 Emily Stewart, "Donald Trump Rode $5 Billion in Free Media to the White House," The Street, November 20, 2016, accessed September 27, 2019, https://www.thestreet.com/story/13896916/1/donald-trump-rode-5-billion-in-free-media-to-the-white-house.html.

6 Margaret Sullivan, "Has the Times Dismissed Bernie Sanders?," New York Times, September 9, 2015, accessed September 27, 2019, https://publiceditor.blogs.nytimes.com/2015/09/09/has-the-times-dismissed-bernie-sanders/?mcubz=0.

7 Max Blumenthal and Rania Khalek, "How Cold War–Hungry Neocons Stage Managed RT Anchor Liz Wahl's Resignation," Truthdig, March 19, 2014, accessed September 27, 2019, https://www.truthdig.com/articles/how-cold-war-hungry-neocons-stage-managed-rt-anchor-liz-wahls-resignation/.

8 Abby Martin, "Abby Martin Responds to Exploitation by NY Times," Media Roots, January 8, 2017, accessed September 27, 2019, https://mediaroots.org/abby-martin-responds-to-exploitation-by-ny-times/.

9 Chris Hedges, "The Myth of the New York Times, in Documentary Form," Truthdig, July 7, 2011, accessed September 27, 2019, https://www.truthdig.com/articles/the-myth-of-the-new-york-times-in-documentary-form/.

10 Chris Hedges, Death of the Liberal Class (New York: Nation Books, 2010), 130.

11   Noam Chomsky, "Noam Chomsky Reads the New York Times—Explains Why 'Paper of Record' Is Pure Propaganda," AlterNet, May 20, 2015, accessed September 27, 2019, https://www.alternet.org/media/noam-chomsky-reads-new-york-times-explains-why-paper-record-pure-propaganda.

AMERICAN SOCIETY WOULD COLLAPSE IF IT WEREN'T FOR THESE EIGHT MYTHS

Our society should've collapsed by now. You know that, right?

No society should function with this level of inequality (with the possible exception of one of those prison planets in a *Star Wars* movie). Sixty-three percent of Americans can't afford a 500-dollar emergency.[1] Yet Amazon head Jeff Bezos is now worth a record 141 billion dollars.[2] He could literally end world hunger for multiple years and still have more money left over than he could ever spend on himself.

Worldwide, one in 10 people only make two dollars a day.[3] Do you know how long it would take one of those people to make the same amount as Jeff Bezos has? One hundred and ninety-three *million years* (if they only buy single-ply toilet paper). Put simply, you cannot comprehend the level of inequality in our current world or even just our nation.

So . . . shouldn't there be riots in the streets every day? Shouldn't it all be collapsing? Look outside. The streets aren't on fire. No one is running naked and screaming (usually). Does it look like everyone's going to work at gunpoint? No. We're all *choosing* to continue on like this.

Why?

Well, it comes down to the myths we've been sold. Myths that are ingrained in our social programming from birth, deeply entrenched, like an impacted wisdom tooth. These myths are accepted and basically never questioned.

I'm going to cover eight of them. There are more than eight. There are probably hundreds. But I'm going to cover eight, because:

- no one reads a column titled "Hundreds of Myths of American Society"
- these are the most important ones
- we all have other shit to do.

Myth No. 8—We have a democracy.
If you think we still have a democracy or a democratic republic, ask yourself this: When was the last time Congress did something that the people of America supported that did *not* align with corporate interests? . . . You probably can't do it. It's like trying to think of something that rhymes with "orange." You feel like an answer exists, then slowly realize it doesn't. Even the Carter Center and former president Jimmy Carter believe that America has been transformed into an oligarchy: a small, corrupt elite control the country with almost no input from the people.[4] The rulers need the *myth* that we're a democracy to give us the illusion of control.

Myth No. 7—We have an accountable and legitimate voting system.
Gerrymandering, voter purging, data mining, broken exit polling, push polling, superdelegates, electoral votes, black-box machines, voter ID suppression, provisional ballots, super PACs, dark money, third parties banished from the debates, and two corporate parties that stand for the same goddamn pile of fetid crap!

What part of this sounds like a legitimate electoral system?

No, we have what a large Harvard study called the worst electoral system in the Western world.[5] Have you ever seen a parent with a toddler in a car seat, and the toddler has a tiny, brightly colored toy steering wheel, so he can feel like he's driving the car? That's what our electoral system is—a toy steering wheel. Not connected to anything. We all sit here like infants, excitedly shouting, "I'm *steeeeering!*"

And I know it's counterintuitive, but that's why we have to vote. We have to vote in such numbers that we beat out what's stolen through our ridiculous rigged system.

Myth No. 6—We have an independent media that keeps the rulers accountable.

Our media outlets are funded by weapons contractors, big pharma, big banks, big oil, and big, fat hard-on pills. (Sorry to go hard on hard-on pills, but we can't get anything resembling hard news, because it's funded by dicks.) The corporate media's *jobs* are to rally for war, cheer for Wall Street, and froth at the mouth for consumerism. It's their mission to actually fortify belief in the myths I'm telling you about right now. Anybody who steps outside that paradigm is treated like they're standing on a playground wearing nothing but a trench coat.

Myth No. 5—We have an independent judiciary.

The criminal justice system has become a weapon wielded by the corporate state. This is how bankers can foreclose on millions of homes illegally and see no jail time, but activists often serve jail time for nonviolent civil disobedience. Chris Hedges recently noted, "The most basic constitutional rights . . . have been erased for many. . . . Our judicial system, as Ralph Nader has pointed out, has legalized secret law, secret courts, secret evidence, secret budgets and secret prisons in the name of national security."[6]

If you're not part of the monied class, you're pressured into surrendering what few rights you have left. According to the *New York Times*, "97 percent of federal cases and 94 percent of state cases end in plea bargains, with defendants pleading guilty in exchange for a lesser sentence."[7]

That's the name of the game. Pressure people of color and poor people to just take the plea deal, because they don't have a million dollars to spend on a lawyer. (At least not one who doesn't advertise on beer coasters.)

Myth No. 4—The police are here to protect you. They're your friends.
That's funny. I don't recall my friend pressuring me into sex to get out of a speeding ticket (which is essentially still legal in 32 states).[8]

The police in our country are primarily designed to do two things: protect the property of the rich and perpetrate the completely immoral war on drugs—which by definition is a war on *our own people*.

We lock up more people than any other country on Earth.[9] Meaning the land of the free is the largest prison state in the world. So all these droopy-faced politicians and rabid talking heads telling you how awful China is on human rights or Iran or North Korea—*none* of them match the numbers of people locked up right here under Lady Liberty's skirt.

Myth No. 3—Buying will make you happy.
This myth is put forward mainly by the floods of advertising we take in but also by our social engineering. Most of us feel a tenacious emptiness, an alienation deep down behind our surface emotions. (For a while I thought it was gas). That uneasiness is because most of us are flushing away our lives at jobs we hate before going home to seclusion boxes called houses or apartments. We then flip on the TV to watch reality shows about people who have it worse than we do (which we all find hilarious).

If we're lucky, we'll make enough money during the week to afford enough beer on the weekend to help it all make sense. (I find it takes at least four beers for everything to add up.) But that doesn't truly bring us fulfillment. So what now? Well, the ads say buying will do it. Try to smother the depression and desperation under a blanket of flat-screen TVs, purses, and Jet Skis. *Now*, does your life have meaning?

No? Well, maybe you have to drive that Jet Ski a little faster! Crank it up until your bathing suit flies off and you'll feel *alive!*

The dark truth is that we have to believe the myth that consuming is the answer, or else we won't keep running around the wheel. And if we aren't running around the wheel, then we start thinking, start asking questions. Those questions are *not good* for the ruling elite, who enjoy a society based on the daily exploitation of 99 percent of us.

Myth No. 2—If you work hard, things will get better.
According to Deloitte's Shift Index survey: "80% of people are dissatisfied with their jobs" and "[t]he average person spends 90,000 hours at work over their lifetime."[10] That's about one-seventh of your life—and most of it is during your most productive years.

Ask yourself what we're working for. To make money? For what? Almost none of us are doing jobs for survival anymore. Once upon a time, jobs boiled down to: I plant the food —> I eat the food —> If I don't plant food = I die.

But nowadays, if you work at a café—will someone *die* if they don't get their super-caf-mocha-frap-almond-piss latte? I kinda doubt they'll keel over from a blueberry scone deficiency.

If you work at Macy's, will customers perish if they don't get those boxer briefs with the sweat-absorbent ass fabric? I doubt it. And if they do die from that, then their problems were far greater than you could've known. So that means we're all working to make other people rich, because we have a society in which we *have* to work, even though technological advancements can take care of most everything that truly must get done.

So if we wanted to, we could get rid of most work and have tens of thousands of more hours to enjoy our lives. But we're not doing that at all. And no one's allowed to ask these questions—not on your mainstream airwaves at least. Even a half-step like universal basic income is barely discussed, because it doesn't compute with our cultural programming.

Scientists say it's quite possible artificial intelligence will take away all human jobs in 120 years.[11] I think they know that will happen, because bots will take the jobs, and then realize that 80 percent of them don't need to be done! The bots will take over and then say, "Stop it. . . . Stop spending a seventh of your life folding shirts at Banana Republic."

One day, we will build monuments to the bot that told us to enjoy our lives and . . . leave the shirts wrinkly.

And this leads me to the largest myth of our American society.

Myth No. 1—You are free.
And I'm not talking about the millions locked up in our prisons. I'm talking about you and me. If you think you're free, try running around with your nipples out, ladies. Guys, take a dump on the street and see how free you are.

I understand there are certain restrictions on freedom we actually desire to have in our society—maybe you're not crazy about everyone leaving a Stanley Steamer in the middle of your walk to work. But a lot of our lack of freedom is not something you would vote for if given the chance.

- Try building a fire in a parking lot to keep warm in the winter.
- Try sleeping in your car for more than a few hours without being harassed by police.
- Try maintaining your privacy for a week without a single email, web search, or location data set collected by the NSA and the telecoms.
- Try signing up for the military, because you need college money, and then one day just walking off the base, going, "Yeah, I was bored. Thought I would just not do this anymore."
- Try explaining to Kentucky Fried Chicken that while you don't have the green pieces of paper they want in exchange for the mashed potatoes, you *do* have

some pictures you've drawn on a napkin to give them instead.

- Try running for president as a third-party candidate. (Green Party candidate Jill Stein was shackled to a chair in a basement by police during one of the debates.)[12]
- Try using the restroom at Starbucks without buying something . . . while black.

We are less free than a dog on a leash. We live in one of the hardest working, most unequal societies on the planet, with more billionaires than *ever*.

Meanwhile, Americans supply 94 percent of the paid blood used worldwide,[13] and it's almost exclusively coming from very poor people. This abusive vampire system is *literally* sucking the blood from the poor. Does that sound like a *free* decision they made? Or does that sound like something people do after immense economic force crushes down around them? (One could argue that sperm donation takes a little less convincing.)

Point is, in order to enforce this illogical, immoral system, the corrupt rulers—most of the time—don't need guns and tear gas to keep the exploitation mechanisms humming along. All they need are some good, solid bullshit myths for us all to buy into, hook, line, and sinker. Some fairy tales are for adults.

It's time to wake up.

NOTES

1   Aimee Picchi, "Most Americans Can't Handle a $500 Surprise Bill," CBS News, January 6, 2016, accessed September 29, 2019, https://www.cbsnews.com/news/most-americans-cant-handle-a-500-surprise-bill/.

2   Zameena Mejia, "Amazon CEO Jeff Bezos Is Now Worth a Record $141 Billion—Here's How He Became the Richest Person in the World," CNBC, June 18, 2018, accessed September 29, 2019, https://www.cnbc.com/2018/06/18/how-amazon-made-jeff-bezos-the-richest-man-alive-worth-141-billion.html.

3   "Just 8 Men Own Same Wealth as Half the World," Oxfam International, January 16, 2017, accessed September 29, 2019, https://www.oxfam.org/en/pressroom/pressreleases/2017-01-16/just-8-men-own-same-wealth-half-world.

4   Akbar Ganji, "The Transformation of American Democracy to Oligarchy," HuffPost, August 6, 2015, accessed September 27, 2019, https://www.huffingtonpost.com/akbar-ganji/the-transformation-of-ame_1_b_7945040.html.

5   Pippa Norris, "U.S. Elections Rank Last Among All Western Democracise," Electoral Integrity Project, January 7, 2017, accessed October 12, 2019, https://www.electoralintegrityproject.com/eip-blogs/2017/1/7/its-even-worse-than-the-news-about-north-carolina-american-elections-rank-last-among-all-western-democracies.

6   Chris Hedges, "The Corruption of the Law," Truthdig, August 20, 2017, accessed September 27, 2019, https://www.truthdig.com/articles/the-corruption-of-the-law/.

7   Erica Goode, "Stronger Hand for Judges in the 'Bazaar' of Plea Deals," *New York Times*, March 22, 2012, accessed September 27, 2019, https://www.nytimes.com/2012/03/23/us/stronger-hand-for-judges-after-rulings-on-plea-deals.html.

8   Crimesider staff, "New Kansas Law Bans Sex between Police and People They Detain," CBS News, May 11, 2018, accessed September 27, 2019, https://www.cbsnews.com/news/new-kansas-law-bans-sex-between-police-and-people-they-detain/.

9   John Surico, "How America Became the Most Imprisoned Nation in the World," *Vice*, October 1, 2015, accessed September 27, 2019, https://www.vice.com/en_us/article/avy474/america-incarcerated-0000765-v22n10.

10 Rachel Premack, "17 Seriously Disturbing Facts about Your Job," Business Insider, August 2, 2018, accessed September 27, 2019, https://www.businessinsider.com/disturbing-facts-about-your-job-2011-2.

11 "AI May Take Your Job—in 120 Years," BBC, June 20, 2017, accessed September 27, 2019, https://www.bbc.com/news/technology-40345188.

12 "Green Party Candidates Arrested, Shackled to Chairs for 8 Hours after Trying to Enter Hofstra Debate," Democracy Now! October 17, 2012, accessed September 27, 2019, https://www.democracynow.org/2012/10/17/green_partys_jill_stein_cheri_honkala.

13 Alexa Valiente, Mark Abdelmalek, and Lauren Pearle, "Why Thousands of Low-Income Americans 'Donate' Their Blood Plasma to For-Profit Centers," January 13, 2017, accessed September 27, 2019, https://abcnews.go.com/US/thousands-low-income-americans-donate-blood-plasma-profit/story?id=44710257.

INDEX

"Passim" (literally "scattered") indicates intermittent discussion of a topic over a cluster of pages.

ABOUT THE AUTHORS

Lee Camp is an American comedian, writer, activist, and host and cocreator of the comedy news shows *Redacted Tonight with Lee Camp* and *Redacted Tonight: VIP* on RT America. He's a former contributor to the *Onion* and a former staff humor writer for the Huffington Post. He has performed thousands of stand-up comedy shows throughout the US and internationally. He's also the creator and host of the web show *Moment of Clarity*. He's the author of *Moment of Clarity* and *Neither Sophisticated nor Intelligent*. His 2018 stand-up comedy special *Not Allowed on American TV* has received rave reviews. He's also the cohost of the weekly podcast *Common Censored* with Eleanor Goldfield. Join Lee Camp's free email list at LeeCamp.com and check out his stand-up comedy special at LeeCampComedySpecial.com.

Chris Hedges is an American journalist, Presbyterian minister, and visiting Princeton University lecturer. His books include: *War Is a Force That Gives Us Meaning*, a finalist for the National Book Critics Circle Award for Nonfiction; *Empire of Illusion: The End of Literacy and the Triumph of Spectacle*; *Death of the Liberal Class*; *Days of Destruction, Days of Revolt*, written with cartoonist Joe Sacco and a *New York Times* best seller; *Wages of Rebellion: The Moral Imperative of Revolt*; and his most recent, *America: The Farewell Tour*.

Jimmy Dore is an American comedian and social critic, host of the hit YouTube show *The Jimmy Dore Show*, and the author of *Your Country Is Just Not That into You*.

ABOUT PM PRESS

PM Press is an independent, radical publisher of books and media to educate, entertain, and inspire. Founded in 2007 by a small group of people with decades of publishing, media, and organizing experience, PM Press amplifies the voices of radical authors, artists, and activists. Our aim is to deliver bold political ideas and vital stories to all walks of life and arm the dreamers to demand the impossible. We have sold millions of copies of our books, most often one at a time, face to face. We're old enough to know what we're doing and young enough to know what's at stake. Join us to create a better world.

PM Press
PO Box 23912
Oakland, CA 94623
www.pmpress.org

PM Press in Europe
europe@pmpress.org
www.pmpress.org.uk

FRIENDS OF PM PRESS

These are indisputably momentous times—the financial system is melting down globally and the Empire is stumbling. Now more than ever there is a vital need for radical ideas.

In the years since its founding—and on a mere shoestring—PM Press has risen to the formidable challenge of publishing and distributing knowledge and entertainment for the struggles ahead. With over 450 releases to date, we have published an impressive and stimulating array of literature, art, music, politics, and culture. Using every available medium, we've succeeded in connecting those hungry for ideas and information to those putting them into practice.

Friends of PM allows you to directly help impact, amplify, and revitalize the discourse and actions of radical writers, filmmakers, and artists. It provides us with a stable foundation from which we can build upon our early successes and provides a much-needed subsidy for the materials that can't necessarily pay their own way. You can help make that happen—and receive every new title automatically delivered to your door once a month—by joining as a Friend of PM Press. And, we'll throw in a free T-shirt when you sign up.

Here are your options:

- **$30 a month** Get all books and pamphlets plus 50% discount on all webstore purchases

- **$40 a month** Get all PM Press releases (including CDs and DVDs) plus 50% discount on all webstore purchases

- **$100 a month** Superstar—Everything plus PM merchandise, free downloads, and 50% discount on all webstore purchases

For those who can't afford $30 or more a month, we have **Sustainer Rates** at $15, $10 and $5. Sustainers get a free PM Press T-shirt and a 50% discount on all purchases from our website.

Your Visa or Mastercard will be billed once a month, until you tell us to stop. Or until our efforts succeed in bringing the revolution around. Or the financial meltdown of Capital makes plastic redundant. Whichever comes first.

Advertising Shits in Your Head: Strategies for Resistance

Vyvian Raoul and Matt Bonner with an Introduction by Josh MacPhee

ISBN: 978-1-62963-574-3
$15.95   208 pages

Advertising Shits in Your Head calls adverts what they are—a powerful means of control through manipulation—and highlights how people across the world are fighting back. It diagnoses the problem and offers practical tips for a DIY remedy. Faced with an ad-saturated world, activists are fighting back, equipped with stencils, printers, high-visibility vests, and utility tools. Their aim is to subvert the adverts that control us.

With case studies from both sides of the Atlantic, this book showcases the ways in which small groups of activists are taking on corporations and states at their own game: propaganda. This international edition includes an illustrated introduction from Josh MacPhee, case studies and interviews with Art in Ad Places, Public Ad Campaign, Resistance Is Female, Brandalism, and Special Patrol Group, plus photography from Luna Park and Jordan Seiler.

This is a call-to-arts for a generation raised on adverts. Beginning with a rich and detailed analysis of the pernicious hold advertising has on our lives, the book then moves on to offer practical solutions and guidance on how to subvert the ads. Using a combination of ethnographic research and theoretical analysis, *Advertising Shits in Your Head* investigates the claims made by subvertising practitioners and shows how they impact their practice.

"Advertising Shits in Your Head *provides a history of the practice (going back to the early '70s), alarming research and theory on the effects of the industry, advice about how to take part (including legal information) as well as several stunning case studies. This is essential reading for all who want to fight back against the 'most powerful and sustained system of propaganda in human history.'"*
—Jamie Kelsey-Fry, *New Internationalist*

Understanding Jim Crow: Using Racist Memorabilia to Teach Tolerance and Promote Social Justice

David Pilgrim with a foreword by Henry Louis Gates Jr.

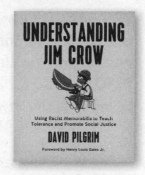

ISBN: 978-1-62963-114-1
$19.95   208 pages

For many people, especially those who came of age after landmark civil rights legislation was passed, it is difficult to understand what it was like to be an African American living under Jim Crow segregation in the United States. Most young Americans have little or no knowledge about restrictive covenants, literacy tests, poll taxes, lynchings, and other oppressive features of the Jim Crow racial hierarchy. Even those who have some familiarity with the period may initially view racist segregation and injustices as mere relics of a distant, shameful past. A a proper understanding of race relations in this country must include a solid knowledge of Jim Crow—how it emerged, what it was like, how it ended, and its impact on the culture.

Understanding Jim Crow introduces readers to the Jim Crow Museum of Racist Memorabilia, a collection of more than ten thousand contemptible collectibles that are used to engage visitors in intense and intelligent discussions about race, race relations, and racism. The items are offensive. They were meant to be offensive. The items in the Jim Crow Museum served to dehumanize blacks and legitimized patterns of prejudice, discrimination, and segregation.

Using racist objects as teaching tools seems counterintuitive—and, quite frankly, needlessly risky. Many Americans are already apprehensive discussing race relations, especially in settings where their ideas are challenged. The museum and this book exist to help overcome our collective trepidation and reluctance to talk about race.

Fully illustrated, and with context provided by the museum's founder and director David Pilgrim, *Understanding Jim Crow* is both a grisly tour through America's past and an auspicious starting point for racial understanding and healing.

Girl Gangs, Biker Boys, and Real Cool Cats: Pulp Fiction and Youth Culture, 1950 to 1980

Edited by Iain McIntyre and
Andrew Nette with a Foreword
by Peter Doyle

ISBN: 978-1-62963-438-8
$29.95   336 pages

Girl Gangs, Biker Boys, and Real Cool Cats is the first comprehensive
account of how the rise of postwar youth culture was depicted in
mass-market pulp fiction. As the young created new styles in music,
fashion, and culture, pulp fiction shadowed their every move, hyping and
exploiting their behaviour, dress, and language for mass consumption
and cheap thrills. From the juvenile delinquent gangs of the early 1950s
through the beats and hippies, on to bikers, skinheads, and punks,
pulp fiction left no trend untouched. With their lurid covers and wild,
action-packed plots, these books reveal as much about society's deepest
desires and fears as they do about the subcultures themselves.

Girl Gangs features approximately 400 full-color covers, many of them
never reprinted before. With 70 in-depth author interviews, illustrated
biographies, and previously unpublished articles from more than 20
popular culture critics and scholars from the US, UK, and Australia, the
book goes behind the scenes to look at the authors and publishers, how
they worked, where they drew their inspiration and—often overlooked—
the actual words they wrote. Books by well-known authors such as
Harlan Ellison and Lawrence Block are discussed alongside neglected
obscurities and former bestsellers ripe for rediscovery. It is a must
read for anyone interested in pulp fiction, lost literary history, retro and
subcultural style, and the history of postwar youth culture.

Contributors include Nicolas Tredell, Alwyn W. Turner, Mike Stax,
Clinton Walker, Bill Osgerby, David Rife, J.F. Norris, Stewart Home,
James Cockington, Joe Blevins, Brian Coffey, James Doig, David James
Foster, Matthew Asprey Gear, Molly Grattan, Brian Greene, John
Harrison, David Kiersh, Austin Matthews, and Robert Baker.